Banishing Burnout

Michael P. Leiter

Christina Maslach

Banishing Burnout

Six Strategies for Improving Your Relationship with Work

JOSSEY-BASS
A Wiley Imprint
www.josseybass.com

Published by Jossey-Bass
A Wiley Imprint
989 Market Street, San Francisco, CA 94103-1741   www.josseybass.com

Jossey-Bass books and products are available through most bookstores. To contact Jossey-Bass
directly, call our Customer Care Department within the U.S. at 800-956-7739, outside the U.S.
at 317-572-3986, or fax 317-572-4002.

Jossey-Bass also publishes its books in a variety of electronic formats. Some content that appears
in print may not be available in electronic books.

Library of Congress Cataloging-in-Publication Data

Leiter, Michael P.
  Banishing burnout : six strategies for improving your relationship with work / Michael P.
Leiter, Christina Maslach.— 1st ed.
      p. cm.
  Includes index.
  ISBN 978-0-470-44877-9 (paperback)
  ISBN 978-0-7879-7608-8 (alk. paper)
  1. Work—Psychological aspects.   2. Psychology, Industrial.   3. Burn out (Psychology)—
Prevention. I. Maslach, Christina.   II. Title.
  HF5548.8.L365 2005
  158.7'23—dc22

                                                                    2004024469

FIRST EDITION
PB Printing   10 9 8 7 6 5 4 3 2 1

Contents

Acknowledgments

We wish to acknowledge the contribution of the many people who completed our surveys, participated in interviews or focus groups, and used these strategies to improve the quality of their work life. The lessons we learned from working with courageous people who care deeply about their work made this book possible.

Chapter One

Your Job and You

Problems at work can hit you hard.

- It hurts so bad.
- I've been done wrong.
- This is not the way it is supposed to be.
- It's driving me crazy.
- I'm mad as hell and won't take it anymore.
- Stop the world, I want to get off.

Sound Familiar?

When you are in a relationship with someone important to you, and things seem to be going from bad to worse, you are likely to experience these thoughts and feelings. "Why isn't this relationship working out? Is it something about me? Or is it the other person's fault? And what can I do to make things right?" The answers to these questions are not always easy to figure out, so trying to cope with a rocky relationship can be frustrating and exhausting.

But suppose it is your *job* that is giving you the blues, rather than a certain someone. Does your relationship with work have any parallels with your relationships with people? As it turns out, the answer is yes. Your relationship with your job is a major part of your life. Indeed you may spend more time with it than you do with friends or family. It demands a lot from you, but it gives you things in return. Your sense of identity and self-esteem may be completely wrapped up in what you do with this job. When a relationship is this important, you want it to be the best that it can be. And maybe you even hope it will be the perfect match, and you will live happily ever after. But the reality is that an important relationship requires a lot of care and feeding—time, effort, commitment, and a dedication to stick with it, both in good times and bad—and that is just as true of your work relationship as your personal relationships.

There are two key players in any relationship: you and the other. In the case of a work relationship, it is you and It (rather than him or her). But even more critical is the connection *between* these two players. When there is a good fit or match between you and It, then you will be engaged with your work. You will be happy, energetic, confident, and ready to commit to a productive long-term relationship. But when there is a poor fit and a major mismatch between you and It, then you will be experiencing burnout. You will be unhappy, exhausted, cynical, and ready to quit and leave It for another job.

Got Burnout?

When burnout hits you, then you've got trouble with a capital T. Burnout is far more than feeling blue or having a bad day. It is a chronic state of being out of synch with your job, and that can be a significant crisis in your life.

- *Burnout is lost energy.* You are constantly overwhelmed, stressed, and exhausted. A good night's sleep is hard to come by, and even then you're soon worn out again. You may try to escape and get away for a while, but when you return, the relationship with It is still as bad as ever. It is very demanding, sometimes unreasonably so, and asks for far more than you are able to give.

- *Burnout is lost enthusiasm.* Your original passion has faded and been replaced by a negative cynicism. Everything about the job rubs you the wrong way: clients are a burden, bosses a threat, and colleagues a chore. The special qualities you brought to the relationship—your expertise, your creative ideas, your sensitivity—have lost their zest and seem to have gone stale. Rather than going the extra mile and doing your very best for It, you just put in the bare minimum.

- *Burnout is lost confidence.* Without energy and active involvement in your work, it's hard to find a reason to keep going. The less effective you feel, the more you will have nagging doubts about your self-worth. When the relationship with It brings you down on yourself, it can be difficult to imagine a way to get out of these doldrums.

Sound bad? You bet. And if you are reading this book, you may already know the personal hurt of burnout all too well. But the impact of your relationship with It has further ripple effects. Your physical health and mental well-being are likely to deteriorate, and you will be more likely to get sick or depressed. The quality of your job performance will decline, and you will become less effective in working with others. The negative vibes of your relationship with It will spill over into your relationships with family and friends and make your entire world a little less bright.

You Are Not Alone

This is not just your problem. You are far from the only one who is feeling this way. In fact, you have lots of company. Burnout is the biggest occupational hazard of the twenty-first century. It's a phenomenon that has been increasing everywhere, creeping into every corner of the modern workplace, growing like a virus, poisoning the increasingly alienated, disillusioned, even angry relationship people today have with the world of work.

- Job stress is estimated to cost the U.S. economy $300 billion in sick time, long-term disability, and excessive job turnover.
- A study by the Harvard School of Public Health concluded that stressful jobs were as bad for women's health as were smoking and obesity. They identified excessive demand, insufficient

decision-making control, and poor personal relationships at work as the major sources of stress.

- Disengaged and unhappy employees cost the British economy almost £46 billion a year in low productivity and lost working days.
- Long-term disability claims based on stress, burnout, and depression are the fastest-growing category of claims in North America and Europe.

These daunting numbers reflect the financial impact but miss the personal impact: people lose the joy and fulfillment that comes from this critical relationship. All of their hopes and dreams for a wonderful life get thwarted or denied. Rather than getting the most out of life, they feel stifled and shortchanged.

So why are so many of us having so much trouble in our relationship with It? The answer lies in the larger context in which that relationship takes place—the take-it-or-leave-it workplace environment of today. As the twentieth century drew to a close, there were already clear signs of a social, political, and economic context in which burnout was becoming an increasingly intense problem. We've made it to the next millennium, but it's difficult to find any examples of improvement.

What's Going On in the World of Work?

The working environment has lost its human dimensions. The following are just a few developments that have an impact on employees' relationships with their work:

1. The corporate world has become more immense and more separated from the concerns of ordinary people than ever before. Mergers and acquisitions flatten corporate cultures into a denominator with which it's difficult to feel common ground. A thriving, independent business becomes a minor operation within a bigger "strategy" or process over which no one seems to have control. A

few people sitting at the top and lurking in financial markets manage to skim incredible wealth from corporations, but the midlevel person, like you perhaps, isn't getting any richer. And worse than that, you're probably feeling unappreciated, underpaid, and exploited by new demands. You're expected to do more and do it faster. You may have lost some benefits, and many around you have lost their jobs entirely. The public sector doesn't hold up much better. Governments merge public sector organizations into larger conglomerates that are increasingly separated from an identifiable community. The control of huge but inadequate budgets consumes more management attention than providing services. Detailed regulations from remote entities determine much of how you spend your workdays. It's not a friendly world out there.

2. Corporations continue to pump up their worth on paper for the short-term gains of a limited few. Strategically placed individuals have amassed incredible wealth by cashing in on the value produced by generations of dedicated managers and workers. Governments, rather than controlling the trend, are following suit. At each level of government, there appears to be a frantic rush to amass debt that will burden generations to come.

3. The outsourcing of services and the exporting of jobs to developing nations continue to disrupt the work world of postindustrialized nations. The difficulties don't stop with the loss of employment in the regions that have lost the work. Communicating with employees in other parts of the world means that work has to get done at times outside the normal nine-to-five schedule, thereby expanding the workday into the work night and the work weekend, and making "24-7" a burden as well as a convenience. Exported jobs are a mixed blessing even for the receiving country. For example, in Guangdong, China, the standard of living of millions of people has deteriorated as their average monthly wage of $50 to $70 has lost its buying power to inflation. At the same time, we're all painfully familiar with how the sustained industrial expansion in China over the past decade is managing to reduce prospects for North American workers who are losing the jobs.

4. It is becoming increasingly evident that some major players in the North American and European economies are capitalizing on the extra-low wages and benefits paid to immigrants of dubious if not completely illegal employment status. These people provide many of the benefits of exported jobs while saving the trouble of exporting them. A few years ago, evidence that someone had employed an illegal alien as an underpaid nanny was the stuff of political scandal. Now, in the corporate sector, it's the way business is done.

5. Information technology continues to produce an array of nifty, entertaining devices of increasing complexity, power, and versatility. In and of themselves, they have the capacity to increase one's effectiveness for dealing with complex problems and to provide excellent, responsive services to one's clientele. But they are intrusive. And over time, their intrusiveness has gotten worse. Cell phones, a required part of life for many occupations, have the capacity to invade our private time and disrupt sleep patterns, upsetting recovery cycles. Furthermore it's getting increasingly difficult to find public areas free of salespeople checking in on prospects or folks just chatting. The convenience of e-mail is undone by the hassles of spam, viruses, and worms. There is an unending list of passwords to remember. And the pervasive and accessible Internet has become a place to waste lots of time through games, diversions, shopping, and exploring information of trivial importance. Although attractive in many ways, computer-based entertainment involves sitting at a screen in a way that is so much like the work setting of many employees that it can hardly function as an effective means of recovery from job demands.

6. Centralization of power in large organizations continues to pull power away from frontline workers. Centralized policies permit a tighter rein on services at the cost of responsiveness. This approach is also evident in governments in North America and Europe, where legislated policies reduce the discretion of government employees to use their judgment to address challenges encountered in their work. Although these policies provide legislators greater confidence that their intentions will be fulfilled, they undermine

the independence of people in a wide variety of occupations, including health care and education.

7. Poor corporate citizenship continues to be reflected in excessive executive compensation. And it emerges in other forms as well. The Enron scandal was the most spectacular example of corporate leadership taking a predatory approach to its dealings with its clients, its stockholders, and its employees. Multinational corporations have become the target of serious political opposition around the world. Some accounting firms have been happy to help these corporations cover their trail. Even though there is a stark contrast between the rampant greed of executives and the inequity that employees have experienced in the form of destroyed pensions, the government has been either unable or unwilling to prosecute the perpetrators of the debacle.

8. Adding unease to work life is the impact of terrorism in North America. The events of September 11, 2001, were an attack on people at work, a large majority in civilian jobs. Going to work became riskier. White powder in an envelope could evacuate a building. Opening parcels could be a bit scary. Orange alerts with vague references to unknown threats, reading like a horoscope on a really bad day, crank up the background anxiety level another notch or two.

9. The security response across the United States and Canada has amplified the impact of the initial attacks. The time, inconvenience, and often the absurdity of airport security checks increase the stress of traveling, as major airlines on the brink of bankruptcy slash the quality of their service. As a demanding, intrusive work demand, business travel is consuming more energy and patience than ever before.

10. The financial requirements of increased security have had a broad impact on public service organizations. As government funds have been shifted to homeland security, international policing, peacekeeping, and wars, then hospitals, schools, and social agencies have been increasingly downsized, while demands for their services continue to grow.

11. News media have figured out that terror gets people's attention, raising their ratings more than other stories. In the increasingly ferocious competition for eyeballs on screens, news programming has become a litany of threats, fears, and actual daily disasters. Terrorists are portrayed as having a vast and complex arsenal of chemical and biological agents to supplement their storehouses of guns, munitions, and black-market thermonuclear devices. And of course there's no lack of horrible images of actual atrocities—huge conflagrations, burning cars and buildings, mutilated bodies, the blood of wounded men, women, and children—all in living color.

12. And there's even more to get you down! From all parts of the globe come new waves of antibiotic-resistant bacteria and deadly viruses, such as SARS. As more people take powerful drugs to solve one problem or another, deadly side effects emerge. Nutrition researchers keep identifying the insidious consequences of eating the food we love the most. Violent crimes and gang warfare are becoming a regular fact of life in many metropolitan areas, and the police have difficulty in bringing them under control. And the list goes on. You can spend hours in front of the television, learning about a treacherous landscape of multifaceted threats to you and all you hold dear.

Given this challenging new world we live in, it is no wonder that our relationship with work is under increasing strain. Everyone is trying to deal with these constantly shifting social, economic, and even ethical issues. But it is at times like these, when things are tough, that it is especially important to have a good solid relationship on the job between you and It. You may hope and pray that It will take the lead in fixing things and making everything all right. And in some rare instances that does happen, as some organizations try to enhance the quality of work life. Unfortunately, other organizations will try to exploit the situation, without concern for the impact on you and other people. But it's most likely that your workplace is just muddling along, doing the best it can under demanding circumstances.

What this all means is that you can't count on It to improve your relationship, so you are going to have to figure out some solutions on your own. And that is the reason for this book: to give you some new understanding of your current state of affairs with It and to give you some new ideas and new tools to make that relationship a whole lot better.

So What's a Person to Do?

This is probably not the first time you have thought about addressing burnout. In a world of health fanaticism—diets, exercise programs, massage therapy, yoga, and thousands of other things that are good for you and sometimes even pleasant to experience—there has to be some way of developing a healthier, less exhausting lifestyle. In a world of meditation, medication, and mediation, there ought to be some way of clearing the mind of cynical, discouraging thoughts. In a world producing a never-ending supply of management fads, there has to be an approach that will increase your self-confidence. Countless individuals, government agencies, and major consulting firms are dedicated to improving your health, your enthusiasm for work, and your potential productivity.

Because you are not the first person to have a difficult relationship with your job, there is already a lot of conventional wisdom out there about what you should do. Let's begin by reviewing some of these tried (but not always true) approaches, so that you can see not only their strengths but also their shortcomings.

Grin and Bear It

One traditional approach to reducing burnout has been to wait until it "goes away," until your work environment happens to evolve into a place that is just the way you like it. This is an easy strategy. It involves no effort, no understanding, and no risk. But you need to ask yourself one question: Am I a patient person? How long am I going to wait for this relationship with It to be just right?

Forever? You may not last that long. Or you might be an entirely different person by the time things come around to how you would like them to be right now. Taking a wait-and-see strategy with It may be no pain, but it probably will also be no gain.

Get Away from It All

Sometimes, when you have had it up to here with It, you need to take some time off. It might involve a long vacation, or it might even involve a trial separation, as when you take a temporary leave of absence. Both of these approaches have some definite pluses. Rest and relaxation on a vacation can help you recover and give you the strength to deal with the challenges at work. Finding some inner peace and pleasure while you are away will help you endure the things that bother you a bit longer than before. Taking a leave may give you a fresh perspective on your relationship with It. You may find that It is actually not so bad, compared with the alternatives out there, or you may discover that your relationship is actually pretty dysfunctional.

But the point is that the job is not going to change while you are away. Everything will all still be there when you return. So despite the advantages of taking a break from It, the downside is that the relationship is not going to get any better. And if it is truly dysfunctional, it will continue to wear away at you. You can't count on holding up for all that long.

Call It Quits

If your relationship with It is really bad, a temporary separation may not be enough. You may opt for a divorce. Leaving It for another can get you out of one bad relationship, but it does not necessarily guarantee that the next one will be better. We will have more to say about this later in the book, when, despite all your efforts to improve the relationship, you may have to face the reality of breaking it off.

It will be important to figure out how to avoid making the same mistakes again, and the tools in this book will help you do that.

In some cases, you may decide to leave It but never look for another. The "alimony" to support you will be a long-term disability claim, given the health costs you have suffered in your work relationship. This is a hard condition for many people. Long-term disability is a solution with a catch, as it defines you as being out of the working world. Once you've been defined as out, ill, disabled, it can be quite difficult to get back in. Even if you find life on disability payments attractive, it is a lifestyle continually at risk of being abruptly terminated by the disability carrier. You lose control of shaping your future. From an individual's point of view, it is a poor solution to burnout.

Set Your Mind Straight

If the relationship with It is getting really bad, and you are suffering from some serious emotional consequences, then you may need to get some therapeutic counseling. Psychotherapy can help you figure out your problems and get you in a state of mind to decide what you are going to do about them. It therefore can be an important first step in recovering from burnout. But the limitation is that the therapeutic treatment is focused on you alone, and not on It. In other words, it is not a form of couples counseling, where both parties in the relationship are trying to work things out.

Figure Out What It's All About

If your relationship with It is going from bad to worse, then you may have to face the big question: "Why are we together?" Is there something special about the work you do that makes it all worthwhile, despite the stressors? A fervently mission-oriented organization, with values that you share, can be an engaging place to work. So various processes for clarifying mission and values can work against burnout by articulating the core goals of the organization and inspiring people to achieve them.

Unfortunately, these values-clarifying processes rarely make it any further than the lofty phrases. To be effective, these values need to be clearly linked to key aspects of day-to-day work life, such as your supervisor's performance evaluation or the reward structure for your work group. But if the mission and values are just a lot of sweet-sounding words and no action, then there is not a very solid foundation for your relationship with It.

Can You Make It Better?

When a relationship is not all that you wanted it to be, there is a natural tendency to seek out what's wrong and point the finger of blame. "The problem is It—It doesn't care. It isn't good enough. It keeps screwing up." Or, "It's all my fault. What's the matter with me? Why do I keep doing this?" Although there may be some cathartic good that comes from blaming you or It, it is not a strategy for making a troubled relationship any better.

Instead you need to focus on what could be right and figure out what changes could get you there. There are three different points where you can leverage change: the two major players (you and It) and the relationship between them.

You Can Try to Change Yourself

One approach is to make yourself a better person. How can you be more effective and a more attractive person for the job? Perhaps if you develop new skills or improve your way of working with other people, you will be bringing more to the relationship with It, and things will get better. There may be training opportunities within your organization, or you can seek out solutions in the variety of self-help books that are available these days.

You Can Try to Change It

Another approach is to make changes in the job. There are some things you can do for yourself (such as negotiate a change in position or responsibilities). Other changes will affect not only you but also some immediate colleagues (such as a process to improve team decision making). These will require you to work collaboratively with those key people.

It is also possible to strive for bigger and better changes throughout the entire workplace (such as more transparent policies for promotions). The challenge here is to revamp the organizational environment in a way that will promote the health and efficacy of all the individuals who work in it. This is no small task, and any initiative to achieve this goal will require the support and effort of many people throughout the organization, from the senior leadership to the rank and file. Such an approach can be daunting, but it can be done. In fact, we have developed just such an organizational strategy, which is designed to provide a checkup of organizational well-being. We describe that approach and provide some of the essential tools in *Preventing Burnout and Building Engagement*. But that organizational approach is not what we are talking about in this book. Rather, we are talking about what you can do on your own.

You Can Try to Change the Relationship Between It and You

The third approach is to focus on the nature of the connection between It and you. Is there a good match, a comfortable fit? Or are you out of synch, experiencing a disconnect? If the relationship is going to work, you will need to figure out how to find a better fit. These solutions may involve better exchanges (you give and you get), as well as better compromises (you win some, you lose some). You will need to recognize what can be changed and what cannot. To achieve a good reality, you may need to let go of some fantasy. Ultimately, you will need to understand why the relationship is important to you and worthy of your commitment. And if it's not, then you may have to face the decision of leaving It for another.

Six Strategies for Improving Your Relationship

So how do you fix a relationship that is on the rocks? When things are bad and heading downhill, you are likely to feel out of control and overwhelmed by it all. And the well-meaning advice you get from friends and family, or from a variety of self-help books, may only add to your feelings of overload and confusion. How do you make sense of this difficult and frustrating situation? What are you ever going to do to make it better? How do you even begin to figure this all out?

The answer lies in the number *six*. Six areas of your relationship with It are where the major trouble spots lie. Six corresponding strategies will help you develop solutions to those problems. And this book will show you how to identify which of those six is the critical starting point for you.

For each of the six *strategic areas*, there is a continuum between a poor and a good match between you and It. The relationship can be a smooth fit or it can be way out of synch. Let's look at each of these strategic areas, in terms of how you might describe your relationship with It.

Workload

A major mismatch in this area of your relationship means that your workload is too much, too complex, too urgent, or just too awful. This overload drives the exhaustion that is at the root of burnout. How do you feel about It in this kind of relationship? You are likely to be saying the following: "It is wearing me out" or "It is asking too much of me" or "It is so stingy, asking me to do too much with too little" or "It is constantly demanding and never gives me a break" or "It lets me down when things get bad."

To deal with this type of mismatch, you will need to use a *work-load strategy*. This strategy will first help you identify which category of mismatch is the biggest problem for you—*exhaustion, excessive availability, time pressure,* or *too much work*. It will then point you to the appropriate objectives for taking action—*resilience, uninterrupted time, time management,* or *reducing workload*—and lay out the steps of your own action plan.

As you make progress in dealing with this mismatch, then you can pace your work in a way that permits you to maintain your best energy throughout the workday. And your relationship with It? Eventually, your reactions will sound something like this: "It makes reasonable demands, pushing me a bit, but not too much" or "Even when It asks a lot of me, It recognizes my limits, and respects my personal time" or "It gives me what I need to do things well" or "When the going gets tough, It makes extra efforts to help and support me."

Control

A major mismatch in this area of your relationship means that you are experiencing problems in authority and influence. Your sense of control over what you do is limited or undermined, and you don't have much say in what's going on at work. How do you feel about It in this kind of relationship? You are likely to be saying the following: "It always tells me what to do and how to do it, as though It knows best and I do not" or "It is always second-guessing me and overruling my judgment" or "It acts like it doesn't need or value my ideas" or "It ignores me."

To deal with this type of mismatch, you will need to use a *control strategy*. This strategy will first help you identify which category of mismatch is the biggest problem for you—*being micromanaged, ineffective leaders,* or *ineffective teams*. It will then point you to the appropriate objectives for taking action—*increasing autonomy, shared leadership,* or *team rehab*—and lay out the steps of your own action plan.

As you make progress in dealing with this mismatch, then you will have the capacity to determine decisions that affect your job and more freedom to work in the way that you think is most appropriate. And your relationship with It? Eventually, your reactions will sound something like this: "It asks for my point of view" or "It supports the choices I make" or "It gives me the liberty to do what I think is best" or "It values what I bring to the relationship at work."

Reward

A major mismatch in this area of your relationship means that you are experiencing problems in the recognition, pleasure, and compensation you get from your job. No part of the job is rewarding or satisfying, and no one seems to notice or care about what you have accomplished. How do you feel about It in this kind of relationship? You are likely to be saying the following: "It takes me for granted" or "It ignores the special things I do" or "It does not really care whether I enjoy what I'm doing" or "It seems to forget about me whenever things are going well."

To deal with this type of mismatch, you will need to use a *reward strategy*. This strategy will first help you identify which category of mismatch is the biggest problem for you—*insufficient compensation, lack of recognition,* or *unsatisfying work*. It will then point you to the appropriate objectives for taking action—*more money, acknowledgment,* or *better job assignments*—and lay out the steps of your own action plan.

As you make progress in dealing with this mismatch, then you will enjoy your work, you will be pleased with the impact it has, and other people will notice your efforts in meaningful ways. And your relationship with It? Eventually, your reactions will sound something like this: "It always lets me know how good I am" or "It recognizes my talents and my potential and pays attention to me" or "It makes life fun and interesting" or "It is proud of me."

Community

A major mismatch in this area of your relationship means that you are experiencing problems in the social community of your job. Whether it is bickering coworkers, patronizing bosses, resentful subordinates, or difficult clients, your social life is full of stress and conflict. How do you feel about It in this kind of relationship? You are likely to be saying the following: "It fails to give me the social support I need" or "It does not help out when there is conflict between me and others" or "It does not know how to handle difficult social situations" or "It isolates me from other people."

To deal with this type of mismatch, you will need to use a *community strategy*. This strategy will first help you identify which category of mismatch is the biggest problem for you—*divisiveness, poor communication,* or *alienation.* It will then point you to the appropriate objectives for taking action—*conflict resolution, improved communication,* or *unity*—and lay out the steps of your own action plan.

As you make progress in dealing with this mismatch, then you are likely to have supportive bosses, friendly coworkers, and subordinates who appreciate your leadership. And your relationship with It? Eventually, your reactions will sound something like this: "It gives me support and understanding" or "It makes it easy for me to have good friends at work" or "It helps me work out problems with other people" or "It promotes teamwork and collaboration."

Fairness

A major mismatch in this area of your relationship means that you are experiencing problems with justice in the workplace. Decisions about schedules, tasks, and promotions are arbitrary and secretive. Favoritism rules, and you are treated unfairly. How do you feel about It in this kind of relationship? You are likely to be saying the following: "It takes unfair advantage of me" or "It fails to give me what I deserve" or "It puts me down and doesn't respect me" or "It cheats on me."

To deal with this type of mismatch, you will need to use a *fairness strategy*. This strategy will first help you identify which category of mismatch is the biggest problem for you—*disrespect*, *discrimination*, or *favoritism*. It will then point you to the appropriate objectives for taking action—*promoting respect*, *valuing diversity*, or *ensuring equity*—and lay out the steps of your own action plan.

As you make progress in dealing with this mismatch, then there will be well-considered and open decisions about resources and authority, and you will be treated with dignity and respect. And your relationship with It? Eventually, your reactions will sound something like this: "It respects me" or "It gives me good reason to trust It" or "It treats everyone fairly" or "It is straightforward with me."

Values

A major mismatch in this area of your relationship means that you are experiencing a significant disconnect in the extent to which you believe in the organization and the organization believes in you. The core values of the organization do not mesh well with yours and may even be irrelevant or offensive to you. How do you feel about It in this kind of relationship? You are likely to be saying the following: "It makes me do meaningless work" or "It is dishonest" or "It acts in ways that I consider wrong or unethical" or "It asks me to accept values that are objectionable to me."

To deal with this type of mismatch, you will need to use a *values strategy*. This strategy will first help you identify which category of mismatch is the biggest problem for you—*dishonesty*, *destructiveness*, or *meaninglessness*. It will then point you to the appropriate objectives for taking action—*maintaining integrity*, *promoting constructive values*, or *adding meaning*—and lay out the steps of your own action plan.

As you make progress in dealing with this mismatch, then your values will be in synch with those of the organization, your work will be especially meaningful, and you will take pride in your workplace. And your relationship with It? Eventually, your reactions will sound something like this: "It asks me to do work of importance" or "It believes in things that are meaningful to me" or "It wants to do the right thing and live up to Its ideals" or "I am proud to be affiliated with It."

How This Book Can Help You Improve Your Relationship

Relationships are varied and complex. And the relationship you have with It is no exception. And it is likely to be somewhat unique and not just like any other relationship with work. After all, there are many kinds of people in the world and many kinds of work environments, so they all will face their own set of challenges when dealing with It. But no matter how varied these relationships are, they can all be understood in terms of the six basic themes—*workload, control, reward, community, fairness,* and *values*. And the six strategies provide a systematic approach for improving everyone's relationship with It.

The starting point for making the relationship better is to be able to pinpoint the areas in which mismatches are occurring. You may be well matched in some areas but experiencing major misfits in others. Knowing your personal profile on the six areas will guide you to the relevant strategy for finding solutions for your problems.

Chapter Two asks a lot of questions to get you to your starting point. Please answer all of the items in the My Relationship with Work Test and then compute your total scores in each of the six areas. Then transfer those scores to the personal profile graph, so that you can easily see the status of the six areas of your relationship with It: which ones are in good shape and which ones are problematic.

Once you have a better understanding of what is going on in your relationship with It, you will be ready to move on to the next stage—to develop an action plan tailored to the strategic areas of mismatch. Chapter Three will lead you through the basics of a generic four-step action plan:

1. Defining the problem
2. Setting objectives
3. Taking action
4. Tracking progress

These four steps will give you a framework for getting on the road to recovery and making the relationship better for you. But be forewarned: an action plan is a long-term process and not a quick fix. Good relationships require time and effort and dedication, and so do the solutions we describe in this book. If you are not prepared to commit to an active strategy of dealing with your problems with It, then this book is not for you.

But if you are ready to take action, then you are ready to follow through with the particular strategy that is linked to the greatest mismatch in your profile. The six strategies, which are presented in Chapters Four through Nine, will apply the basic four-step framework to the targeted action plans for each of the six strategic areas. Multiple options will be presented in each chapter, and you are encouraged to develop additional possibilities that are especially relevant to your particular situation. Each chapter has forms for you to use to articulate the various steps and time line for your plan and to note your progress toward your goal. There are also tips on how to do it right (and how to avoid missteps), as well as examples of what other people have done to make their relationship with It a success.

After you develop your specific action plan on paper, then you need to make it a reality in your work life. This will take time, during which your use of this book will be focused primarily on keeping track of your progress and making necessary modifications along the way. (After all, even the best-laid plans are rarely perfect.) There are two important points to keep in mind:

- Relationships are complicated things, so there is no single solution, no magic bullet, no one-size-fits-all approach. You will need to be flexible and creative.

- Relationships do not change all that easily, so reaching your long-term goal calls for insight, planning, and persistence. You will need to be patient and optimistic.

Eventually, your plan will take effect, and some changes (however small) will occur. At some point in the future, you will want to return to this book and check in on how things are going in your relationship with It. When you are ready to take the My Relationship with Work Test again, you will find it waiting for you with a blank form at the end of the book, in the section called Checking Up. You can either check in on how things are going with your current relationship or assess the viability of a new one.

In sum, this book presents a guide to addressing burnout against all odds. The challenge is to find a way of furthering your personal agenda for work in a less-than-completely-friendly environment. We realize that you cannot change this environment all by yourself. But you can learn to manage it more effectively, sidestepping some pitfalls, and turning dubious situations to your advantage.

Your relationship with It is a critical part of your life, so let's figure out how to make it the very best it can be.

Chapter Two

What Is My Relationship with Work?

This chapter begins the process of defining your current relationship with It by generating a profile of the six strategic areas. Your job in this test is to give a critical evaluation of every component of your current job, in terms of the degree of "fit" or "match." For every question, you will be asked to indicate whether things are "just right" (that is, a good fit), a "mismatch," or a "major mismatch." Be picky! Don't say something is just right unless it really is. Your comparison reference in this test is your ideal work situation (and not what you will put up with just for the sake of being reasonable).

My Relationship with Work Test

Once you've taken the test, you'll have clarity on which areas of your work are a match, which areas are a major mismatch, and which areas are just right.

- In each of the six areas, how does your current job fit with your preferences, work patterns, and aspirations? If things on a given dimension are just right, put a check in the Just Right column.
- If a certain dimension is incompatible with your preferred way of working, put a check in the Mismatch column.
- If a quality is a major departure from your ideals, put a check in the Major Mismatch column.

The six tables that constitute the My Relationship with Work Test (Workload, Control, Reward, Community, Fairness, and Values) follow.

Workload

This section is about the work. The items focus on the amount of work, the kind of work, the pace of work, and the demands of work. These items call for a fairly long-term perspective. The issue isn't today's workload but the state of things over the past few months and how you expect things to be in the foreseeable future.

		Just Right	Mismatch	Major Mismatch	Score
	Rating	0	1	2	
W1	The amount of work to complete in a day				
W2	The complexity of my work				
W3	The intensity of demands from customers				
W4	The firmness of deadlines				
W5	The frequency of surprising, unexpected events				
W6	The opportunity to settle into a comfortable groove				
W7	The frequency of interruptions in my workday				
W8	The proportion of my work time spent with customers				
W9	The amount of time I work alone				
W10	The amount of time I work with other employees				
	Workload Total				

Control

This section focuses on the environment for making decisions at work. The items concern the amount of authority you can exercise over your job and over the operation of your work group. For these items, it doesn't matter how you've gained this authority. You may be empowered by company policy or you may have gained influence through your personal networking. The issue is about providing an accurate reading of your capacity to make decisions about your work.

		Just Right	Mismatch	Major Mismatch	Score
	Rating	0	1	2	
C1	The amount of group decision making in my work setting				
C2	The extent to which I share authority with coworkers				
C3	The amount of information my supervisor provides on major developments in the organization				
C4	My participation in decisions that affect my work				
C5	The quality of leadership from upper management				
C6	The quality of leadership shown by my immediate supervisor				
C7	The authority I am assigned in my area of responsibility				
C8	Opportunities to exercise my professional judgment				
C9	My capacity to influence decisions that affect my work				
C10	My freedom to follow my professional judgment				
	Control Total				

Reward

This section is about rewards. There are many ways a job can be rewarding and just as many ways that it can miss the boat. For this section, give some thought to the sorts of things that keep you going.

		Just Right	Mismatch	Major Mismatch	Score
	Rating	0	1	2	
R1	My salary and benefits relative to what I require				
R2	My salary and benefits relative to what I could get elsewhere				
R3	Recognition for achievements from my supervisor				
R4	Recognition for achievements from management other than my supervisor				
R5	The rigorousness of regular performance evaluations				
R6	My access to perks at work—travel, office furniture, conference support, and so forth				
R7	Opportunities for promotion				
R8	Opportunities for bonuses or raises				
R9	The amount of time I do work I truly enjoy				
R10	The amount of time I work with people I truly enjoy				
	Reward Total				

Community

The focus in this section is the people who make up your *social work environment* (hence the designation S on the test, which distinguishes it from the C used in the control section). Think of the people you encounter on the job: clients, coworkers, bosses, subordinates, and others.

		Just Right	Mismatch	Major Mismatch	Score
	Rating	0	1	2	
S1	The ease of discovering what is happening across the organization				
S2	Open, honest communication across the organization				
S3	The freedom to express differences of opinion				
S4	The extent people must rely on others at work				
S5	The frequency of supportive interactions at work				
S6	The closeness of personal friendships at work				
S7	The amount people interact informally at work				
S8	A shared sense of purpose across the organization				
S9	My sense of community with the entire organization				
S10	The extent of openness to people from units other than one's own				
	Community Total				

Fairness

This section focuses on respect and fairness. Think of the important decisions that affect the quality of your work life. How are people around you treated, and how do you treat others? To what extent are fairness and respect evident in the life of your company?

		Just Right	Mismatch	Major Mismatch	Score
	Rating	0	1	2	
F1	My supervisor's attention to treating employees fairly				
F2	Upper management's attention to treating employees fairly				
F3	Management's dedication to giving everyone equal consideration				
F4	Clear and open procedures for allocating rewards and promotions				
F5	Procedures for discipline that are specified in detail				
F6	The objectivity of decisions on pay raises or bonuses				
F7	The objectivity of decisions on work schedules and assignments				
F8	The extent to which individuals interact politely and respectfully				
F9	The level of cultural sensitivity across the organization				
F10	The organization's accommodation of diverse backgrounds and abilities				
	Fairness Total				

Values

Do you believe in what you're doing? This section is about the way your values and those of your company fit together. Or don't. Think of the crunch issues that pit one set of values against another. Does the company come through for you? Does the company come through for its own corporate values?

		Rating	Just Right 0	Mismatch 1	Major Mismatch 2	Score
V1	The depth of management's commitment to its mission					
V2	The influence of organizational values on my work					
V3	The influence of the organization's values in everything it does					
V4	The level of honesty across the organization					
V5	Management's diligence in maintaining honesty and integrity					
V6	My willingness to make personal sacrifices in order to further my organization's mission					
V7	The potential of my work to contribute to the larger community					
V8	My confidence that the organization's mission is meaningful					
V9	The constructive impact of the organization's mission and activities					
V10	The organization's contribution to improving the general quality of life					
	Values Total					
	Grand Total					

Scoring

Scoring the test gives you a Total for each of the six strategic areas. Here's what you do:

- For each of the six sections, put a check in the cell under either Just Right, Mismatch, or Major Mismatch for each item. Then enter the Rating number (0, 1, or 2) into the right-hand Score column for each item.
- Add up the scores within each strategic area and put the total score in the Total cell. This will give you six Total scores, one for each strategic area.
- In the Grand Total row at the bottom of the test, enter the sum of the six Total scores and then divide by six.

Profile

Now you have the information to plot your personal profile, which will provide the strategic direction for your action plan. This profile is a unique map of your relationship with work. The person at the next desk might come up with a similar map, because you both experience the relationship in the same ways, or that person might have a strikingly different perspective that describes a world you barely recognize. That's because you're not mapping the physical work environment, showing how the chairs and tables are positioned. You're mapping your own psychological relationship with work. This personal profile reflects *your* thoughts and feelings about the critical elements of your work setting. Other people have their own unique take on their world.

For each of the six Total Scores, find the corresponding number on the scale along the left side of the graph (see figure that follows). Fill in the rectangle for each strategic area to the height corresponding to the score. The score can range from a low of 0 (indicating everything is just right) to a high of 20, indicating a major mismatch on every item for that particular strategic area.

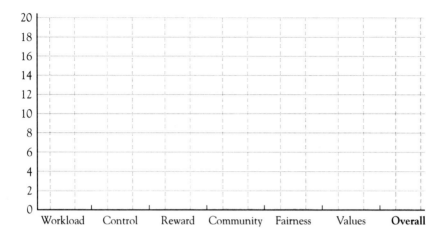

Sample Profile

The completed graph (see the following figure) indicates that the largest mismatch for one individual is in the strategic area of Control, whereas Community has the smallest mismatch. By averaging the scores, you arrive at an Overall mismatch of 8.

Using the Profile

Your profile will guide your work throughout the rest of this book. It defines the shape of the critical six strategic areas of your work

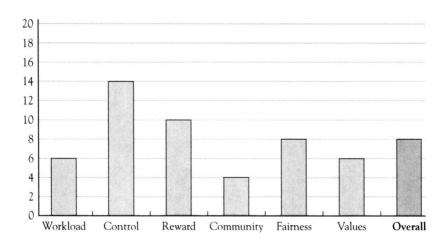

relationship: some areas will be working well for you, but in others there will be elements that impede your personal growth. Your profile identifies the trouble spots that are pushing you toward burnout. In doing so, it also points to the specific strategy that will lead you toward a productive and fulfilling engagement with It.

Your personal profile is a reference point for your progress. At critical times during the implementation of your action plan, you'll want to return to the My Relationship with Work Test to generate a new profile. (An extra copy of the test is available in the Checking Up section at the back of the book.) The changes between now and then will track your success in bringing your work life in line with the way you work most effectively.

Onward!

Your personal profile defines the challenge before you. You knew you had issues with It, which require some serious work, and now you should have a better sense of the strategic area that needs attention. But you want to go beyond this initial insight and figure out what to *do* about the problem, right? It's all about taking some serious action to make your relationship better, and the next chapter will show you how to go about doing just that.

Chapter Three

Making a Plan of Action

You're tired of waiting. Despite your pleas and complaints, nothing is happening to make things better. So if your situation on the job is going to get any better, if your sense of burnout is going to diminish, then it's up to you. You're on your own, and you're going to have to take charge of your work life.

Taking charge is not for the faint of heart. If you want things to be better, then you have to commit yourself to taking action (and not just griping about how bad things are). This requires time, effort, and courage. And you have to hope that a better future is indeed possible. Even when the going gets tough, or there are setbacks, you need the optimism to keep carrying on. This sense of hope and optimism, this confidence that you can make a difference, on your own, is crucial.

The greatest challenges in your work life are alleviating burnout and building engagement with work. When your efforts are successful, you improve things for yourself and your employer. Addressing these issues is of such critical importance that you would think every business would invest seriously in helping employees address them. But few even try. And those that try seem to give up easily. The limited scope and effectiveness of organizational initiatives to address these challenges is disappointing. In rare instances, employers come through with the support systems, job design, and mentoring that you need to master the demands of your career. But for the most part, time and again, the company does too little if anything at all.

We have been working for years advising organizations with insightful, courageous leaders who strive to enhance the quality of work life for their employees. And we are aware that we're touching only a few of the thousands of workplaces that could use some help.

You're on your own out there.

This chapter is about how to take charge of your work life. The following section lays out a four-step program for using the results of your My Relationship with Work Test and your personal profile to address mismatches in any of the six strategic areas. It describes each of the steps, noting the critical points for each. It then emphasizes the importance of a constructive attitude to the project's success.

Four Steps to Take Control of Your Work Life

By implementing the following steps, you will be able to take control of your work life. In the chapters that follow, we'll show you how to apply these steps to each of the six work areas in your life.

1. Defining the problem
2. Setting objectives
3. Taking action
4. Tracking progress

All along the way, you'll need to check out the situation, track your plan's impact, and revise on the spot, as needed.

Step One: Defining the Problem

The first step is defining your problem through a series of questions.

What Area of Work Life Is a Problem?

Scan the results of the My Relationship with Work Test. The strategic areas with the larger scores are your problem areas. A high score results from having many mismatches; a very high score results from having many major mismatches. Although things may not be perfect in the other areas, they're relatively better, so ignore those for the time being. You can save ironing out the fine points of those strategic areas for another day.

What Are the Specific Problems Within That Area of Work Life?

Within each area of work life, you can encounter distinct problems. Part of defining the problem is defining it more specifically and narrowing it down to a manageable proportion. For example, a workload problem may be that the physical workload is so great that you're exhausted and experiencing back strain. Or it could be that there is too much work to complete in a workday, requiring you to take work home, allowing it to interfere with your personal life. Or it could be unreasonable deadlines requiring you to work flat out too much of the time, introducing a level of franticness in to your life. Any of these problems can represent a workload mismatch.

When defining the problem, your scores on specific items of the My Relationship with Work Test will help specify the problem. For example, the fourth item under Workload, W4, refers to the firmness of deadlines. If that is the only major mismatch in this area, it suggests that deadlines are the issue.

The more specifically you drill down to define the problem, the more workable you'll find it. A general problem—"I feel miserable"— true though it may be, is not something you can address directly. "I have too many firm deadlines that I can't meet" defines a more workable problem.

Step Two: Setting Objectives

Having identified a specific and manageable problem in one of the six basic areas of work, you can begin the process of formulating a goal, a remedy, an ideal solution, a direction to go toward.

Make Very Specific Choices

You set objectives by defining your preferred alternative. You have to make some choices, because there are a variety of alternative solutions for just about any problem.

General or vague objectives, such as "improving my work life," make it hard to assess progress. A strong action plan defines goals so that you can identify each and every small gain. Progress is often slow and subtle. A small gain may be quite meaningful; you don't want to miss it.

In terms of the My Relationship with Work Test, a measurable improvement is moving some items rated as a major mismatch to mismatch and some mismatches to just right. For example, in day-to-day life, the first step in improving a work life problem where you feel unappreciated may be any sign that your supervisor has noticed your contribution.

Be Positive, Be Practical

Emphasize the positive: an effective plan needs positive objectives. It's not enough to get away from a bad situation. You need to be going somewhere. For example, a good objective regarding feeling exhausted would go beyond eliminating fatigue to identifying an energetic state to take its place. It goes beyond knowing that your work is unrewarding to identifying the fulfilling experiences you hope to bring to your work. It goes beyond reducing meaningless drudgery to identifying the meaningful activity that would ideally dominate your work.

Recognize what's practical: focus on what's doable. You are not going to convert the entire company away from the profit motive through this program, but you may gain freedom to pursue some of your personal values through your work. You're unlikely to change your ambitious, tight-fisted boss into a relaxed, supportive mentor very quickly, but you can hope to gain acknowledgment for your accomplishments. You cannot eliminate all deadlines from your life, but you can get some relief from incessant, unreasonable time pressures.

In approaching your work with definite objectives, you are taking control. You are designing a fulfilling work life.

Step Three: Taking Action

Plans are nothing without action.

You have defined a problem that you'd like to put behind you.

You have set an objective toward which you want to strive, which requires an inventory of techniques and strategies.

Action Strategies

Determining which action strategy is the best depends on how you have discovered your problem and defined your objectives. Here are some key action strategies. They encompass diverse approaches, all of which come together to produce a better match between you and your work setting.

Engaging in Self-Development Activities. Some action plans you can take on your own. On your own, you can develop skills and capabilities that will help you in your work. The challenge is to have the discipline and persistence to develop your skills and abilities sufficiently to apply them to your work. For example, one component of addressing problems with deadlines is to enhance your time management skills. This approach would be appropriate if one source of your deadline problem was an inability to prioritize a long list of demands. You could target your time management skills to improve your capacity to set priorities. Another example is overcoming exhaustion by increasing your stamina through personal exercise and physical training.

Exerting Your Influence. Some action plans involve having an impact on colleagues, supervisors, or other people at work from the start. Their actions, systems, or attitudes are the target of your intervention. Changing what they do or say is a condition for the plan's progress. A critical part of the plan is determining the best way to influence them. The possibilities include subtle hints, en-thusiastic sales pitches, reasoned arguments, leveraged demands, and ultimatums.

For example, your objective of managing deadlines more effec-tively could target a project manager as a common source of unrea-sonable deadlines. One element of your action strategy, therefore, can be persuading this person to accommodate your overall work demands when assigning you time-limited tasks within the team's projects.

Taking Initiative.   In a third kind of action plan, you go di-rectly to action. You don't discuss, suggest, or negotiate anything with anybody. You just start doing your work differently, in a way that is a better match for you. These action plans may start with a self-development phase, building the capabilities you need to work differently. Or you may already be fully capable of working in the new mode. You may already have the skills, power, and leverage to plunge ahead.

An essential part of an initiative strategy is your preparation to deal with any objections that colleagues or management may raise about your change in work patterns. For example, having mastered a time management system, you begin prioritizing your work based on your assessment of the relative importance of your work de-mands. Instead of reviewing these priorities with your supervisor, you begin working according to *your* priorities, and you are prepared to address any objections along the way.

Exercising Leverage.   In being persuasive, your first line of de-fense (or attack) is the logic of your arguments. But you have other qualities that add leverage to your arguments. Your potential for leverage is in the background whenever you attempt to exercise in-fluence. In some strategies, leverage may be more explicit.

One source of leverage is your expertise and experience. As a highly valued employee, you can exercise more influence than can a less experienced colleague of more dubious status. Other sources of potential leverage include external reputation (famous people have more clout) or professional associations. Contacts outside the organization, such as a long list of loyal clients, add to leverage. Contacts within the organization, especially with people in important positions, are another asset. And of course, the ultimate leverage is the outside offer that permits you to leave if you don't get what you want. Speaking of which . . .

Giving an Ultimatum. In most cases, it is possible and desirable to effect meaningful change, to work around the problem, or to negotiate more reasonable working conditions. In most cases, but not in every case. Sometimes it comes down to an ultimatum. Before contemplating confrontational strategies, consider the following checklist:

- Have you exhausted milder approaches?
- Can you afford to lose? A poorly resolved confrontation could jeopardize your job security or generate problematic hostility. Do you have an alternative source of employment?
- What suggests that confrontation will work?

  Have you had success with confrontation?

  Have others in this work environment had success with ultimatums?

  Are you confident that the company recognizes your value to the company and wants to keep you on board? That is, are you working from a strong position?

A careful review of these points is an essential preparation for delivering an ultimatum. This is a high-risk approach. It could be your only viable option. It could bring big returns. But it's risky.

So how serious are you about changing the pace of your work assignments?

If the deadline pressure is so intense that it's jeopardizing your health and well-being, if the organization is being unresponsive to your requests, and if you have other career options, then—after a reasonable attempt at negotiation, influence, and leverage—your ultimatum is this: lighten up or I quit.

It might just do the trick.

But be ready for the company to accept your ultimatum.

In all of these strategies, the focal point is your behavior. Your behavior includes your persuasive abilities, which are the starting point for *influence action plans*. It includes the actions and routines you build into your life to pursue *self-development action plans*. It includes changes in your work patterns that make up your *initiative action plans*.

Targets: What Has Impact?

To reach your objectives in the future, you change what is happening now. The targets of your actions are the processes, relationships, or structures that are getting in the way. If your objective is to gain more recognition of your accomplishments, then likely targets are colleagues within your team, your immediate supervisor, and people in more senior management positions. The targets are what you want to influence to reach your objective. To select a target, you consider whose recognition is important to you and whom you have the best chance to influence.

A good target is one that has a big potential for impact. A small change in one person's attitude, one workplace routine, or one organizational policy will reverberate impressively. Here's an example: if your objective is building a stronger team spirit in your work group, you will get more mileage from influencing individuals who are opinion leaders in the work group. If your objective is reducing deadline pressures, you will have a greater impact focusing on the project manager who sets the time lines. In planning interventions, you're always looking to change the element that has the greatest potential impact on your problem and the greatest potential to help you reach your objective. You are one person; it's a big organization you're trying to change. You're not going to get there by brute strength. You need to carefully select a few targets that will have a big effect.

My Relationship with Work Test

Your scores on the test help you cut through the complex web of influences, structures, and barriers at work to select the issues that would lead to the most effective improvements in your work life. Consider the items with your biggest mismatches. These define charged issues that are clearly out of balance in your work life. For example, if your reward mismatches concern your intrinsic satisfaction from your work (R9 and R10), then your most effective targets are the people and processes that assign your tasks.

What Are the Hot Topics?

Another perspective on having impact comes from other people in the organization. Note what your colleagues identify as the hot topics. It might be power, money, or expertise. It may be that the boss gets bonuses each time the team exceeds the previous quarter's production levels. The focus of their attention will help you understand what makes things happen within the organization. When your plan successfully targets a person or process that makes things happen in the organization, you have a greater chance for enduring impact.

What's Doable?

A leverage point won't do you any good unless it's doable. The last thing you need is a brick wall to bang your head against. You can do a lot to improve your situation, but some objectives—although meaningful—are long shots. If you're working in a government office that has instituted a wage freeze, getting a significant raise in your salary has a low probability of success. It's best not to go there as a short-term objective, although improving your financial rewards remains a legitimate objective in the longer term.

Here's another example: your long-term goal is to reduce the amount of work you take home over the weekend. But the workday is filled with so many meetings that you have to leave the office to get anything accomplished. To simply stop taking work home can leave you far behind the pace of things at the office. So you need a more doable, immediate target. One immediate target is to eliminate meetings on Fridays, so that you have a chance of completing major assignments before the weekend. On the way to eliminating Friday meetings, the plan considers ways in which your group can complete its work at other times during the week. By moving back from major issues beyond the control of an individual, the plan identifies more modest targets that are more susceptible to your influence.

An effective plan starts with readily doable short-term objectives. Success is encouraging. It also is informative. If you encounter brick walls on your way to modest objectives, you have learned something about your company's responsiveness. You may find that you have a lot of freedom to change some aspects of your work life but very little latitude in other areas. This information will help shape a plan to develop a relationship with work that is fulfilling for both you and your employer. You have to stay on your toes, attend carefully to how It receives your initiatives, and be ready to adapt to the reality of your situation. The flexibility in your design is a real asset.

Step Four: Tracking Progress

It's important that you track your progress carefully. A small, subtle improvement may be significant, especially when there appears to be little hope for significant meaningful change. Tracking includes brief notes on what you have tried and how others have reacted. It also includes returning to the My Relationship with Work Test to reassess the matches and mismatches in your life. Fill in and update the blank Action Progress Form (Table 3.1) to track your progress as you complete the four steps. In Chapters Four through Nine, you'll see sample Action Progress Forms that have been completed. They address in specifics the six strategies for improving your relationship with It.

Table 3.1. Action Progress Form

Area of Work Life: _____
Problem: _____

The Objective	The Target	Actions	Time Line	Progress
1.		• • •	• • •	• • •
2.		• • •	• • •	• • •
3.		• • •	• • •	• • •

What is the area of work life where your numbers are highest? How have you identified the problem in a way that is manageable? Where are you going? Identify your long-term objective. And what is your action plan, in a nutshell?

What is your time line? Write target dates for each project. Indicate when you expect to take action, when you hope to see some initial progress, and when you hope to reach your long-term objective. Leave room on the time line for notes and revisions: you can't anticipate everything that will happen in your work world, so you have to be ready to revise along the way. Important developments often take a bit longer than you anticipate.

Tracking progress helps. It reminds you of what you did and why. It gives an indication of how you're moving forward. The record doesn't need to be anything fancy. Just notes on a time line.

General Guidelines

Here are some more tips to keep in mind as you work through your four-step program for each of the six areas of work.

Anticipate Resistance to Change

Your situation at work probably has a lot of inertia. By the time you notice a serious mismatch on workload, you may have settled into a strained relationship with your organization.

- Your company or organization expects you to continue performing.
- Your supervisor and colleagues may show little concern for your feelings of exhaustion, cynicism, or discouragement.
- It may be hard for anyone else at work to imagine that you have a legitimate complaint.

The work, pacing, and interactions of other people fit around your current mismatched relationships at work. Your current uncomfortable situation is being reinforced and perpetuated by everything happening around you. Breaking out of that pattern is a big deal. Without action on your part, it just keeps rolling along, with little concern for your feelings.

Any change in your activity will throw things off a bit for others. Your newly designed action plan will require them to adapt—maybe a little, maybe a lot. The excellence of your newly designed work life may not be at all appreciated. There will be pressures—some subtle, some not so subtle—to get you back to your previous patterns, to not rock the boat. Resisting that pressure while redefining yourself as a vibrant, productive part of your work world is an integral part of any plan.

For example, if your time management analysis identifies a specific behavior as low priority, there are likely to be interests who believe those activities *are* very important. They will then work on influencing your priorities. If your boss gets a bonus every time the unit does more with less, you're going to encounter a lot of resistance to your plans for slowing down.

The flip side of this resistance is the power of the same work environment to perpetuate your new work design once it is established.

Sometimes small changes in your day-to-day routine can help you make bigger changes in your relationship with work. A change in where you work or how you interact with others can help you establish new ways of doing things: such as adjusting your workload. These strategies follow your overall approach of identifying problems, setting objectives, and taking action; they include specific actions that might not have occurred to you.

The strategies outlined in the following sections are not intended to be a complete, comprehensive list. We have covered a broad range of approaches. Some may be exactly appropriate to your situation; others may require some modification on your part to fit into your work world. There may be other qualities of the work situation that you can change as part of your approach to addressing serious mismatches.

Build Alliances

Any strategy has an opportunity to work with others. You are not alone. Others around you are struggling with very similar challenges.

Your goals have room for collaborating with other people to further mutual interests. The approach used in this book encourages you to consider potential allies for initiatives you develop.

You can use all the help you can get. In your work life and in your personal life, there are people who wish you well. There are people who share many of the same frustrations and hopes that you experience. Connecting with others can help you make your plan wiser. You might even find others willing to take action to improve their relationship with It. There is potential here for emotional support as well as practical advice. A shared adventure is simply more fun.

Assess Your Risks

Action always carries risk. Our approach encourages you to consider the potential pitfalls of any initiative. It considers risks to your productivity, job security, and well-being. You should be fully aware of every risk you take.

Before beginning a journey, think about the dangers. Your present situation is far from perfect. The idea is to improve what's not working, not put everything in jeopardy. Your current position is not only a viable source of livelihood, it is also your best base for moving on to another position, should you decide to leave your current job. Employed people are more attractive job candidates than unemployed people. So, for many reasons, putting your job in jeopardy requires serious consideration.

Risk assessment goes beyond protecting your job security. Some actions can compromise other career focuses: your chances for promotions, your opportunities for enjoyable work, personal relationships with coworkers, or your freedom to incorporate your values into your work. Initiating change in your work life is always a risky thing to do. The idea is not to avoid all risks, but to recognize and accept the risks you are taking from the outset.

Stay Positive

In addition to these strategic steps, our approach encourages a proactive attitude toward your efforts.

- *Develop a bias toward action.* Our approach addresses challenges at work with ingenuity, persistence, and decisiveness. Making decisions is your way of moving past challenging and undefined situations at work. This is not the lazy man's guide to enlightenment. It requires thought, effort, and courage.

- *Maintain an optimistic attitude.* Your experiences with burnout are discouraging. That discouragement in itself slows you down. Part of any action plan is a positive attitude. You have a bright future. You move past disappointments, frustrations, and setbacks, learning from the experiences but not lingering on them. Fully recognizing the downside of a disappointment, you return to your optimistic perspective for the next step. Regardless of how grumpy you feel right now, you pump yourself up for this challenge. You have hope.

- *Remain centered.* You are the primary resource for this plan. It all rests on your ability to get to the bottom of complex problems, define reasonable goals, identify powerful leverage points, and see through a plan to action. It takes courage, pace, and staying power. Put into it the preparation and focus required of running a marathon or climbing a really big mountain. You can't squander your energy and enthusiasm in the first ten minutes.

But with persistence, dedication, and close attention to the approach presented in the following chapters, you will see it through. And success will reward you with a more fulfilling life at work.

Chapter Four

Solving Workload Problems

Any lively organization generates more demands than you can fulfill. In an information economy, people are constantly flooded with information, reading material, and learning opportunities. In a service economy, customers maintain high expectations on the quality of service, its timing, and customization. In a regulatory environment, government agencies and professional associations maintain an incessant need for data, forms, and reports. There is enough to keep you constantly reacting to demands. Putting your own direction on your work life these days requires extra focus, special effort, and definitive action.

If your profile has a major mismatch in the area of workload, you must act to deal with what you have to do, how much has to get done, and where, when, and how fast you have to get it done. The answer isn't always doing less work, but it is always doing your work differently. Being overloaded by unreasonable, unmanageable, or unbearable demands is exhausting and discouraging. Your challenge is transforming these pressures into sustainable life at work. To do this, you need to choose a strategy that fits your career aspirations, your personal talents, and your work situation.

So let's go through the four-step program and see how you can solve problems in the area of workload.

Step One: Defining the Problem

So you have a high score in the area of *workload*. But what exactly is the problem? How would you define it in a way that is understandable, manageable, and capable of leading to an objective and plan of action?

Even though you may be painfully aware of the problem, it may be difficult to translate it into a framework that promotes action. You know how bad you feel when you fall behind schedule, gloss over important details, ignore opportunities for personal contact with clients, or allow work to interfere with your personal life. The point here is for you to learn to translate your experience of the problem into a workable problem.

In terms of the My Relationship with Work Test, note on the form the workload items on which you scored mismatch or major mismatch. Bigger scores mean bigger problems. The content of the specific items on which you are experiencing your mismatches identifies the dimensions of workload that are especially aggravating.

In light of your scores on the My Relationship with Work Test and your experience of the mismatch, write a brief description of your workload problem. Here are some examples that we will explore in this chapter.

Workload Problem: Exhaustion

The experience of exhaustion reduces your initiative while progressively limiting your capacity for demanding work. One of the definitive signs of burnout is feeling exhausted in the morning when facing another day on the job. Chronic exhaustion means low resilience. You don't have the stamina, fortitude, and toughness to withstand the demands.

Indications in the My Relationship with Work Test. Exhaustion is a general problem associated with excessive workload. It inhibits your capacity to take charge of your workload. It inhibits your capacity to take advantage of this book.

Exhaustion is implied by mismatches or major mismatches on any or all of the items on the workload section (W1 to W10).

Workload Problem: Being Too Available

Some of us are just too available for too much work. We're too present, too willing, and too able. People can sense this and start piling on more responsibility. Too much comes our way too easily.

Indications in the My Relationship with Work Test. Excessive availability is unsatisfying and unsustainable. And it is entirely too common in today's work world.

Excessive availability is implied by mismatches or major mismatches on items W3, W5, W6, W7, W8, W9, and W10. These items indicate excessive time being directed by others and insufficient time establishing your own work pace.

Workload Problem: Not Enough Time

Time runs out too soon. It seems to be going faster and faster as the days, weeks, and months rush by. We feel as if we can't keep up, we can't catch up, it's overwhelming, and it may ultimately defeat us.

Indications in the My Relationship with Work Test. Time pressures reflect a poorly regulated work life. This makes you anxious. And it too is entirely too common in today's work world.

Time pressure is implied by mismatches or major mismatches on items W1, W2, and W4. These items indicate insufficient time to do what needs to be done.

Workload Problem: Too Much Work Assigned

You are constantly assigned more work than you can manage. You're discouraged, exhausted, and constantly vulnerable to criticism for failing to have everything done.

Indications in the My Relationship with Work Test. Time pressure is implied by mismatches or major mismatches on items W1, W2, W3, W4, and W5. These items assess your experience of overall workload demand.

These are a few of the potential problems you might identify if you have a high score in the area of workload. The problem now is where to start. How can you best address the pain, inconvenience, annoyance, and aggravation of having too much work? The next step is identifying objectives: What is going to take the place of the problem?

Step Two: Setting Objectives

Having defined workload problems, the next step is defining what it is that you want to take their place in your work life. Within the My Relationship with Work Test, the matter is quite straightforward: replace major mismatches with mismatches; replace mismatches with just rights. So let's consider various ways to confront the kinds of problems just discussed.

Workload Objective for Exhaustion: Resilience

A great and wonderful alternative to exhaustion is resilience. We are able to build up our capacity to persist in demanding situations. Regardless of your success at improving your quality of work life, you are able to increase your physical strength and stamina to the point where you can withstand a higher level of demand and tolerate more frustrations without succumbing to exhaustion. For example, an individual who has an active involvement in a fitness program that emphasizes strength and flexibility is less likely to experience back strain on the job. The capacity to relax deeply and quickly in a work situation is an effective buffer to psychological strains at work.

There are other potential objectives in dealing with the problem of fatigue and exhaustion: reducing the amount of work, producing less, working overtime, and taking an extended vacation. Choosing the best approach depends on factors in your work life and your personal life. Your personal life may not tolerate your spending more hours at work. Or you may anticipate that working overtime will only result in more work being assigned. You may not have the vacation time for an extended vacation, or the company may discourage employees from making full use of the time they have. All of these considerations go into selecting an approach for addressing exhaustion. But regardless of whether or not any of these are the best or only solutions to your particular version of exhaustion, being physically fit can help in whatever objective you ultimately determine should be the way to approach the problem.

Workload Objective for Being Too Available: Creating Uninterrupted Time

When you're pushed and pulled by excessive availability, you'd like some time that is out of the flow of demands to work on projects or tasks. Periods of work time when you can count on freedom from interruptions allow you to establish your personal pace. They allow you to focus on a single topic rather than be pulled by external demands in all directions. They allow you to complete something rather than perpetually juggle multiple tasks, none of which ever get done. They make your work demands more manageable.

Workload Objective for Not Enough Time: Improving Time Management

Being able to move efficiently through your work demands, setting priorities, and attending to time lines can enhance your capacity to stay ahead of the demands of an intense work life. Making the most of the finite amount of time, energy, and talent that you bring to your work requires a concerted strategy. The world is full of distractions that can squander your time. The nature of your work constantly evolves, leaving previous time management solutions obsolete soon after you work them out. It's a constant challenge and there is always room for improvement.

Workload Objective for Too Much Work Assigned: Reducing Workload

The most direct approach to dealing with too much work assigned is to negotiate a reduced workload. This objective is doable if you can make the case that the workload is unreasonable, that you can produce within a reasonable level of expectations, and that you are an asset to the company.

Alternatively, the company can provide resources—training, support staff, technology—that can lead to a more manageable re-arrangement of your work demands. The key is developing a new pattern of workload that permits you to address the key demands. A catch is that new resources can be demanding as well. Training programs are time-consuming. Support staff require direction. Technology requires a learning curve and a certain amount of maintenance. It takes careful planning to ensure that additional resources actually reduce your workload.

These four objectives are examples of states that are positive contrasts to the workload problems identified in the previous section. Although many people experience these problems, workload mismatches provide other forms of distress. With the Action Progress Form as a guide, you can define objectives for other problems, following this format.

Step Three: Taking Action

Taking action calls on a mix of creativity, problem solving, and courage. This section provides general guidelines for taking action and examples of how people have used these guidelines to address problems with workload. Usually, a single intervention is one piece of a broad strategy to take control of your work life. Rarely does a single action, clever and well considered as it may be, radically change your day-to-day work life. But taking these actions over time builds a distinct and improved relationship with the company.

In each case outlined in the following discussion, we'll suggest an action plan based on a specific objective resulting from your definition of the manageable problem.

Workload Objective: Resilience

Resilience is a mix of physical well-being and positive attitude. It is a quality that gets you through the tough stretches. Resilience combats the most definitive and debilitating quality of burnout: exhaustion. Although increasing your resilience does not make you immune to all work demands, it does increase the range of demands, disappointments, and tough situations that you can endure. Even more important, the systems you put into place to increase your health and perspective lay the foundation for taking control of your work life.

By reflecting on your state of health and well-being, you can define the kind of program that would be helpful to you. Possibilities include aerobic exercises, sports, strength building, relaxation, meditation, counseling and other mental health programs for improving emotional resilience, and many more. At times, these programs are best complemented with treatment for chronic illnesses.

Start a Personal Fitness Program. It's not difficult to find a local gym or fitness center or Y that's convenient and relatively inexpensive. Your research can include talking with friends, reading promotional materials, and taking advantage of one-week trial offers. The immediate target is to participate on a regular basis until your activity enhances your resilience.

Promote a Workplace Fitness Program. Many companies and organizations have on- or off-site programs designed to enhance health primarily through physical exercise and nutrition. Employees are often encouraged to use these programs because of their convenient location in the workplace, a cost advantage of a subsidized program, and the opportunity to exercise with friends. Health initiatives also include improving dining options for on-site dining facilities or vending machines. If they are not available, instituting them may be an effective target for action.

Participate in an Emotional Resilience Program. In many lines of work, emotional exhaustion is a greater risk than physical exhaustion. The emotional demands of providing services to demanding clientele or providing leadership in a dynamic corporate environment can be daunting. There are workplace programs available on developing emotional resilience and *emotional intelligence*—the capacity for emotional sensitivity being present in a constructive way at work. Alternative approaches include meditation, massage, or exercises designed to develop calm and centeredness.

See Table 4.1, which illustrates an action plan for implementing the objectives discussed in this section.

Workload Objective: Creating Uninterrupted Time

Time on your own to pursue projects can be hard to come by in many circumstances. But one advantage to this strategy is that you don't need to make other people do anything except leave you alone. The targets for gaining uninterrupted time are often focused on the people, processes, and routines that keep you too easily available to others. Here are some potential action plans to achieve this objective.

Changing Spaces. You may benefit from a bit more distance. If you spend your workday in the line of fire—the first face your boss sees when something's got to be done; the first person a client sees coming through the door—then consider moving. Finding an attractive alternative space can present a serious challenge, requiring persuasion and leverage on your part. It requires convincing whatever authority controls space allocations that you have a good reason to improve your work space.

Table 4.1. Action Progress Form

Area of Work Life: Workload
Problem: Exhaustion

The Objective	The Target	Actions	Time Line	Progress
1. Developing pacing and resilience	Start a personal fitness program.	• Identify community programs. • Set a regular fitness time. • Select an ongoing program.	• 2 weeks • 2 weeks • 4 weeks	• • •
2. Developing pacing and resilience	Promote a fitness facility at work.	• Identify potential programs. • Assess interest among coworkers. • Present concept to management. • Present concept to occupational health office.	• 2 weeks • 2 weeks • 4 weeks • 8 weeks	• • • •
3. Developing pacing and resilience	Participate in an emotional resilience program.	• Identify community programs. • Set a regular fitness time. • Select an ongoing program.	• 2 weeks • 2 weeks • 4 weeks	• • •

Trading Off.   Another strategy for opening project time is to trade off with colleagues. A coworker covers your contacts for an hour or for a morning while you pursue a project at work, and you cover for that coworker the next day. You're doing double duty in exchange for some breathing room.

Being Flexible with Work Hours.   If you have options for flexibility in your work time, then arriving extra early can open uninterrupted time. This only works if you're a morning person—actually able to produce focused work in the early morning. It also has to fit within the morning routines of your personal life and commuting. But if those conditions work, it can open uninterrupted time on a regular basis.

For example, Betty, an emergency room nurse, wants to devote time to a project to develop a better waiting room facility for young children, who often spend hours at the hospital while a parent or sibling is awaiting and receiving treatment. In the day-to-day flow of an ER facility, uninterrupted time is hard to come by. She worked out an exchange with another nurse on the same shift schedule. Each would cover for the other for two one-hour periods each week. This exchange gave Betty the opportunity to do the groundwork on the program, which was launched after six months of concerted effort.

See Table 4.2, which illustrates an action plan for implementing the objectives discussed in this section.

Workload Objective: Improving Time Management

The time-pressured life is stressful. Your good intentions to deliver projects on time or respond to client requests promptly are overwhelmed when there is just too much to do. But it just might be that you're less than totally efficient. That's where time management comes in: it assumes that you could do a better job of managing what comes your way.

Table 4.2. Action Progress Form

Area of Work Life: Workload
Problem: Being Too Available

The Objective	The Target	Actions	Time Line	Progress
1. Creating uninterrupted time	Change work space.	• Identify alternative locations. • Tailor persuasive arguments for relocation. • Present arguments.	• 2 weeks • 2 weeks • 4 weeks	• • •
2. Creating uninterrupted time	Trade off duties with colleagues to create project time.	• Identify potential projects. • Tailor persuasive arguments for engaging in the projects. • Present arguments.	• 2 weeks • 2 weeks • 4 weeks	• • •
3. Creating uninterrupted time	Explore working at different times.	• Identify best working times. • Rearrange schedule. • Assess impact of change.	• 2 weeks • 2 weeks • 4 weeks	• • •

Stop Wasting Time.   The contemporary workplace offers lots of ways to waste time. Computers are a snake pit of diversion. Employees in networked workplaces waste an astounding amount of time surfing the net. Every Windows system comes packaged with games to lead the undisciplined down the pathway of time wasting. (Most unlikely last words: "I should have spent more time playing Minesweeper.") Word processing programs permit you to format reports and reformat colleagues' reports so that they look very crisp and spiffy. But how much of that formatting is consequential?

Ineffective computer use can gain near addictive status. You know it's bad for you but you just can't stop. You produce rationalizations on how it really helps you relax. (Let's get this straight: To relax from your job sitting in front of a computer screen all day, you sit in front of a computer screen?) It is time to take an inventory of your computer use, noting the time wasters, and eliminating them from your workday. By the way, in Windows under Control Panel is Add or Remove Programs, which uninstalls any diversionary software. Constraining Web surfing and e-mail monitoring within a limited daily schedule may also enhance your productivity.

Prioritize.   If you've got more work than you can do or that you can do on time, prioritizing ensures that you can do the important tasks first. The management development world is awash in time management systems. Implementing a systematic approach to managing your time can reduce the clutter of your workday, allowing you to focus directly on issues that matter to you and to others in your work life. An important consideration in choosing among the vast array of systems available is finding one that you can sustain over the long run.

You start the process of enhancing your time management skills by researching the options. There may be training sessions at your work, the local community center, or college. Selecting a system depends somewhat on what's available. Other considerations are cost and complexity: some programs are built on technology and paraphernalia; others can be implemented on a calendar book. Some are so complex that they present challenging conceptual puzzles; others are dead simple. Some only work well within a work team initiative; others work fine as individual initiatives. Considering the various qualities, you can find a system that can help you manage your time more effectively.

Delegate. Your effectiveness is limited by your capacity to delegate. That capacity is defined by your personal style: if you're committed to controlling all the details, you're reluctant to hand important work off to others. That capacity is also defined by the quality of your staff: Do they have the skills and judgment to handle major responsibilities?

You can expand your capacity to delegate through a step-by-step process of developing your staff's potential. This approach builds a more capable and committed team. Your direct involvement in developing their potential gives you a good idea of the level of responsibility you can assign to each member of your staff. When successful, a well-thought-out delegation strategy means that your time and availability are no longer the bottleneck in your operation.

The steps begin with identifying each person's potential through performance evaluation and career planning. You move from closely monitoring the projects you assign to allocating a wider span of control to employees, consistent with their development.

See Table 4.3, which illustrates an action plan for implementing the objectives discussed in this section.

Workload Objective: Reducing Workload

Reducing your workload in a time of doing more with less is a challenge. But it may be essential to your ability and willingness to continue with your job.

Persuasion. Persuading your boss to give you a break from demanding work for project work requires a clear rationale. There are rationales with greater chances of success:

Table 4.3. Action Progress Form

Area of Work Life: Workload
Problem: Not Enough Time

The Objective	The Target	Actions	Time Line	Progress
1. Improving time management	Stop wasting time.	• Identify issues determining scheduling constraints. • Identify positive scheduling trade-offs. • Present arguments.	• 3 weeks • 2 weeks • 2 weeks	• • •
2. Improving time management	Prioritize.	• Identify potential approaches. • Set single daily priority. • Implement time management system.	• 2 weeks • 2 weeks • 4 weeks	• • •
3. Improving time management	Delegate.	• Assess staff's potential. • Closely monitor delegated projects. • Allocate greater responsibility.	• 2 months • 6 months • 2 years	• • •

- *Quality.* A more reasonable pace of work will permit you to deliver work of greater quality.
- *Sustainability.* A more reasonable pace of work will permit you to stay with this job for the long term, enhancing your skills and deepening your contribution to the company.
- *Fairness.* A more reasonable pace of work is consistent with the expectations for other employees.

The objective is to find a point of mutual benefit. You and the company stand to gain from a more reasonable pace of work assignments. The potentially charged element of negotiating job assignments calls for preparation. Prepare a proposal of what seems workable, pointing out how it differs from the current state of things. Acknowledge the plan's costs as well as its benefits. This interaction will call upon your capacity for influence and leverage.

Skill Development. New skills can help you manage your existing workload. For example, project management software could eliminate the detail work that is associated with laying out a project schedule and keeping members of the project team on the time line.

Key considerations in a skill development strategy are the following:

- *Is this really a time saver?* Some software solutions produce sharper-looking reports but don't really save any time. You just spend your time doing different things. And although a change might be nice for a while, the point here is reducing your workload.
- *What is the training time?* If you're already overloaded, then fitting a major training program into your life is a problem. New point-and-click software is one thing; a major database management program that is a significant new demand in your life is quite a different thing. The overall plan needs a means of getting relief while you learn the new skill.

Skill development allows you to repackage existing work. You're able to maintain the bottom-line productivity while reducing workload.

Support Staff. If the workload is unsustainable and the company requires the work to be done, additional staff is an option to consider. If the work to be done translates directly into additional revenues, then a cost analysis can determine whether additional staff are justified. If it is determined that the additional work is not creating significant additional revenue, it may not be all that important.

Revenue generation is not the primary determinant of activity in a nonprofit or government office. The potential productivity of additional staff members is weighed against other uses of the organization's staff or funds. You can make a case for reallocating the work of existing staff members to assist in your work. Or you could propose an increase of funds to your department to employ new personnel.

See Table 4.4, which illustrates an action plan for implementing the objectives discussed in this section.

General Guidelines

Consider the following guidelines for solving workload problems.

Anticipate Resistance to Change

Resistance is predictable. By anticipating opposition to your plans, you can address it before it slows you down.

- Developing the space and the time for project work may appear as a diversion from your primary job. You can anticipate this potential criticism with a clear explanation of your objectives. Working with others on such an initiative also lessens the appearance of losing your focus.

- Attempts to influence or reshape the scheduling process may appear as exceeding your authority. Recruiting others in such an initiative may appear as fomenting rebellion. You can

Table 4.4. Action Progress Form

Area of Work Life: Workload
Problem: Too Much Work Assigned

The Objective	The Target	Actions	Time Line	Progress
1. Reducing work demands	Persuasion	• Develop rationale. • Prepare for meeting with supervisor. • Negotiate reduced workload.	• 3 weeks • 2 weeks • 2 weeks	• • •
2. Reducing work demands	Skill development	• Develop rationale. • Determine training programs. • Complete training. • Implement new skills.	• 3 weeks • 2 weeks • 6 months • 6 months	• • • •
3. Reducing work demands	Support staff	• Develop rationale. • Prepare cost analysis. • Make persuasive presentation. • Employ staff.	• 3 weeks • 2 weeks • 2 weeks • 3 months	• • • •

reduce this risk by approaching the individual responsible for scheduling early in the process to explain your intentions and present the initiative in a positive light.

- Your staff may resist your attempts to delegate. If they perceive you to be more committed to handing off your responsibilities than to developing their potential as individuals or a team, they may not cooperate enthusiastically.

- Your boss may flat out refuse to negotiate a reduction in work-load. The unit is under pressure to produce and there is no one else to do the work. You may find yourself immediately evaluating whether an ultimatum is a feasible option.

Build Alliances

Your success will improve with alliances. The projects described in this section have distinct opportunities for recruiting support.

- You could recruit friends from work (or elsewhere) to join you in a personal fitness program for building resilience. Even if you initiate such a program, you are likely to find like-minded people along the way.

- Individuals with responsibilities for occupational health and safety are likely allies for your initiatives toward promoting workplace fitness programs.

- Developing the space and the time for project work goes more smoothly when working with others. Members of a group have the capacity to cover for one another when individuals are unavailable to respond to clients or queries.

- Scheduling is sometimes an intensely competitive undertaking. A plan for getting a jump on everyone else in your work team is likely to prompt countering actions quickly. A shared initiative to enhance the scheduling system all around has a better chance for long-term success.

- Time management is a learning experience. The technologies involved, such as computer-based scheduling software, are designed for work groups, not just individuals. As a group undertaking, a time management initiative has the potential for helping everyone.

Assess Your Risks

The best-laid plans developed with the best of intentions can backfire. Awareness of potential risks gives you a greater potential for anticipating and addressing them.

- Becoming more fit has few downsides. But it is advised if you are quite out of shape to get advice on the pace and type of exercise that best suits you. In addition to medical doctors, there are trainers in just about any field to advise you.
- Promoting an employee health program at work may appear as a diversion from your primary job. You can anticipate this potential criticism with a clear explanation of your objectives. Working with others on such an initiative also lessens the appearance of losing your focus.
- Time management has few risks other than the danger of developing a system so elaborate that it takes too much time and energy to manage.
- Negotiating a reduced workload may identify you as an uncommitted employee. In many organizational cultures, management advancement and executive positions assume extraordinary workweeks: long hours, weekends, extensive travel. There is a risk of defining yourself out of competition for these positions.

Step Four: Tracking Progress

In some situations, your progress may be obvious. But sometimes you have to look closely to assess progress. And sometimes you need an accurate record to remember how different things used to be.

Are things improving? Along the way, it is useful to record your implementation of the action plan and reactions of clients, coworkers, managers, and the company in general to your initiatives.

In the final column of the Action Progress Form, note the dates on which you implemented each of the steps.

An Illustrative Story

After a long day of taking Walter and his managers through the process analysis of his plan for the branch of an international manufacturer of automobile equipment, all the while systematically sidestepping their sensitivities to criticism, Karen felt overwhelmed by her workload. She was eager to settle in to the privacy, the quiet, and the isolation of her bland, characterless hotel room.

It was so nice being alone. Although she was tempted to fade into whatever distraction could be provided by TV dramas or get lost in the intricacies of the novel that accompanied her travels, Karen instead found herself thinking about her life and her work.

Something was wrong. That much was clear from her feeling of being exhausted whenever it was time to go into the report phase of a project. Karen loved her work. It wasn't like her to cringe. This wasn't a work life situation that Karen wanted to tolerate for long.

The work pace was throwing her off balance by constantly invading her personal life. Although her job may have been enough for a complete life a couple of years ago, Karen now had other life priorities that her workload and travel schedule were disrupting. Karen wanted her life back, which meant having the capacity to make decisions about how she would spend her time.

Karen had taken the My Relationship with Work Test and had discovered that her workload mismatch was about people. The company expected Karen not only to conduct the analysis but also to communicate it to managers. From the company's perspective, the analysis was only a step toward the real objective of improving management. From Karen's perspective, analysis was enjoyable; dealing with defensive people was not. She disliked the tense confrontations that invariably followed her recommendations for improving operations.

Following the Four Steps

Here's how Karen worked the four steps.

Step One: Defining the Problem: Too Much Work Assigned

Karen didn't have to reflect a long time to know that dealing with difficult people was a major mismatch for her.

Indications in the My Relationship with Work Test. Karen scored major mismatches on W3, W8, W9, and W10. In completing those items, she thought of the managers with whom she worked as her customers as well as her coworkers. The mismatch was that there was too much time spent with them and not enough work time alone.

Step Two: Setting Objectives: Reducing Workload

Karen's objective was to negotiate a reduction in her workload. She reasoned that the company could be satisfied with her written reports and could inform managers that they had to get on with implementing her recommendations. This would eliminate the tense, awkward meetings for Karen. Alternatively, the company could create a new position, someone to work with managers, interpret Karen's reports, cool down the managers, and deal with follow-up calls.

Step Three: Taking Action: Skill Development and Acquiring Support Staff

Karen prepared her arguments thoroughly, calculating the costs of the additional staff person, balancing them against the potential savings that her work generated. She laid out her arguments in detail to her manager, Bill.

After an extensive discussion, Bill pointed out that a problem with Karen's preferred resolution was that it fails to appreciate how managers learn and develop. If they're going to change, managers have to actively participate in the process. They need to be convinced that Karen's recommendations are in their interests. Being convinced was going to come from discussions, not from reading a report. If they can't talk with Karen, they'll want to talk with her boss, not her assistant.

Bill proposed an alternative objective: Karen could learn to master if not enjoy the people demands of her job within a self-development strategy. Through training or mentoring, Karen could gain the confidence and skills necessary to provide feedback, defuse defensiveness, resolve conflicts, and refine her reports through direct dialogue with managers. This approach fulfills the company's expectations. It also furthers Karen's long-term ambitions for senior management positions. Advancement in a corporate environment requires a capacity to deal with tense interactions with people.

This solution was consistent with Karen's career ambitions but would add to her workload. She couldn't imagine fitting an extensive executive development program into her already overloaded work life. After further discussion, Bill committed that the company would reassign the responsibilities of a secretary in his office to assist Karen with managing her workload. If this reassignment worked well, the position could be upgraded on an ongoing basis as an executive assistant. This position would also develop a capacity to conduct similar reviews when Karen was ready to advance to more senior positions. He also committed to regular meetings with Karen for mentoring on people management.

Step Four: Tracking Progress

A year later, Karen had attended workshops on leadership and win-win negotiation techniques. Managing the feedback process with the branch plants was the primary focal point of her briefing meetings with Bill after each site visit. And items W3, W8, W9, and W10 were no longer major mismatches. She actually looked forward to meeting the challenge of the feedback sessions.

Chapter Five

Solving Control Problems

When control's the problem, you're not the one making things happen. Rather than acting, you're being acted upon. It's frustrating and demeaning. Too many demands make you tired, but this makes you mad. You deserve the authority that comes with respect. You've earned it. Your experience and commitment to this organization ought to be worth something.

Step One: Defining the Problem

When *control* is the problem, you are ignored, manipulated, uncertain, and frustrated. Rigid policies and petty bureaucrats overrule your expertise and judgment. Weak, ineffective dolts fill leadership positions whose potential they lack the courage to fulfill. They undermine your confidence and block your capacity to lead a meaningful work life. It's so frustrating to be ignored. You have a lot to offer that's going to waste.

The bottom line is that you need more authority over your work.

Control Problem: Being Micromanaged

Being micromanaged is a serious aggravation. Your supervisor wants to tell you what to do every minute of the day. You may be required to do countless reports and forecasts; then new reports and re-forecasts; reports, re-forecasts; reports re-forecasts. You're not allowed to make any decisions on your own or to spend time the way you see fit. Every action, every moment of your workday, is closely planned, monitored, and evaluated—all by someone else, not you. You're not in control. It's enough to drive one mad, and it's so unnecessary, because the net result is spending a lot of time worrying about how you spend your time and *not* spending time doing what is creative and productive in your work.

Micromanagement is a pervasive blight upon the work world. It reflects a misplaced confidence in the wisdom of central control. Along the way, it weakens employees' commitment and potential.

Indications in the My Relationship with Work Test. Micromanagement is indicated by mismatches on C7, C8, C9, and C10.

Control Problem: Ineffective Leadership

In some workplaces, you may find yourself in a one-to-one relationship with a supervisor who seems to you to be incompetent and wrongheaded. You wish your supervisor were a good leader; everyone wants a capable and competent boss, but in this case, it's obvious to you that for whatever reason this person is not up to the job.

When people in positions of authority fail to provide good leadership, the work environment is uncertain and you lose control over managing your work life. Failures in leadership may result from failings of the individuals in positions of responsibility or from organizational policies that undermine their efforts to function effectively. In either case, you have a challenge before you.

What's really aggravating is that weak leadership and micromanagement go hand in hand. Rather than backing off, giving employees the latitude to follow their judgment at work, weak leaders want to dictate the details. They're in your face—not with inspiring leadership but with interference.

Indications in the My Relationship with Work Test. Ineffective leadership is implied by mismatches or major mismatches on items C5 and C6.

Control Problem: Ineffective Teams

In some workplaces, you're in a team with four or five other individuals. It may be a team that's been together for a long time and has taken an unexpected downturn in cooperation, collaboration, or productivity. In other cases, it may be a team that's just started working together or has a bunch of new members and hasn't yet co-alesced or gotten up to speed in an effective manner. In any of these cases, the problem is that you find yourself not in control.

Indications in the My Relationship with Work Test. An ineffective team is implied by mismatches or major mismatches on items C1, C2, C3, and C4.

The problem in all of these situations is that you're in the not-in-control group. Your lack of autonomy and exclusion from important decisions deny your full participation in the company. They dim your future prospects and make you angry.

The next challenge in identifying objectives is this: What is going to take the place of these problems?

Step Two: Setting Objectives

You want to have control. You want the freedom to exercise your own power, test your skills, and stretch your limits. You want your colleagues to respect your judgment, ask your opinion, and collaborate within an effective team. Simple. These really do seem to be reasonable requests. They would fit well in an organization that has confidence in its employees and an unswerving commitment to its mission.

Control Objective for the Problem of Micromanagement: Increasing Autonomy

The first objective is to push back the constraints of micromanagement to open your capacity to follow your judgment and to make meaningful decisions about your work.

Increasing your autonomy is a fundamental objective in managing your work life. It plays a pivotal role: a reasonable range of autonomy permits you to make real decisions about other aspects of your work life. People who are tightly micromanaged have a tough time making big changes at work.

Increasing autonomy means making more decisions of greater scope or impact than the ones you have previously made. For example, an account manager at a bank is delegated the authority to approve loans up to a designated value based on an explicit set of criteria. Rather than leaving the client sitting alone while going to the branch manger for approval, the account manager makes the decision. This mode of operation increases the account manager's confidence and builds stronger customer relationships.

Control Objective for the Problem of Ineffective Leadership: Shared Leadership

If you have a weak leader, you have an opportunity to volunteer your own skills and support. To be well received, you need to offer your assistance in a way that does not threaten this individual. Although you can't fix it all in one fell swoop, you can make a modest contribution to the quality of leadership in your organization by finding a way to contribute, making a creative plan that divides the responsibility, even within the current hierarchy, without rocking the boat.

Specifically, you can persuade your supervisor that you can help. You can offer to do things that are currently left undone, like creating new systems or products, coordinating liaison with other departments, and evaluating your current agenda and proposing a more effective process, a more realistic goal, or greater quality control.

For example, without being critical of your supervisor, you might volunteer to prepare a report on the state of your current process. This report would propose new initiatives that give you a major new role. Through your help in filling a leadership gap, you increase your control and contribute to the leadership of your operation.

Shared leadership is a vast improvement over no leadership at all.

Control Objective for the Problem of Ineffective Teams: Team Rehab

When you're working as an individual under one supervisor, moving strategically into a greater responsibility for evaluating current activities and creating new goals is an effective way to take on more control. But if you're working in a team, you need an approach that fits this different context.

Teams are like families. They may be tightly knit, mutually respectful, and highly productive. . . . Or they may be dysfunctional, contentious, and counterproductive. In such cases, your objective has to focus on the specific problems that you've identified. For example, a new member of the team may be having trouble integrating with the old hands. Or a failure of communication between key players may have created an impasse that must be mediated. Or there may be a profound difference of opinion regarding strategy, techniques, or ultimate goals. Part of being a well-functioning team is the capacity to move smoothly and quickly through these problems. But without effective problem-solving processes, the team becomes stuck, leaving team members feeling not in control. When focusing on the team, the objective is to develop a situation in which each member feels some control and is confident that the team is contributing to everyone's mutual benefit.

Increasing your control over important aspects of your work is to change your relationship with the company and the people with whom you work. One dimension of increasing control is reducing the extent to which others determine the way you work. Another dimension is building alliances, especially members of your work team that empower the group to work effectively *as* a group.

The next challenge is identifying targets for your action plans.

Step Three: Taking Action

The major targets for building control are the processes, people, and procedures that affect consequential decisions in the organization.

They are where things may branch in one direction or another. It can be as mundane as choosing the color to paint an office wall or as lofty as articulating the core values of the organization. At some point, these decisions get made. Or a decision is made to avoid making a decision. Or a decision is made to do nothing and let things evolve on their own. To reach an objective of greater control, you get closer to those decision points.

Control Objective: Increasing Autonomy

In a micromanaged situation, you're spending too much time on the trivial end of the scale, reacting to the insane and compulsive needs of an obsessive boss. Everything you do is being directed by this supervisor. Here are some strategies in response.

Micromanage Back.   So your boss is trying to call everything you do every minute. But his only source of information about what is happening is likely to be *you!* So one tactic is to manage your informational reports to him in terms of what you think are the priorities. Identify the data and events that are of higher priority and lead to the agenda you wish. Play the same game. In other words, by micromanaging back to your supervisor in a manner that gives you control over the information he's using, you also get more control over his decision-making process and directives to you.

Push the Limits of Your Control.   The essence of this approach is acting as if you have a bit more authority than you usually have. If all goes well, you may find that you actually have a bit more latitude than you thought. Avoid sensitive areas that are sure to prompt a response from above. For example, start small. As the manager of a store within a retail clothing chain, you receive directives from central office on window displays for the store. It specifies the brands and styles to be displayed. Within a detailed list of specifications, you have authority over details of color and accessories. You'd like to push the boundaries.

Build Control with Performance. A more gradual approach to increase your freedom of action in a tightly monitored environment is to build your credibility within an influence strategy. Management prefers to be in control of things. It's what management does. In persuading those in authority to allocate more authority in your direction, it helps to establish that you have the ability, character, and willingness to make good decisions. There are strategies for building that credibility.

A record of exceptional accomplishment and sound decisions gives the power of expertise. Your actions communicate that things work out much better when you have the freedom to follow your judgment.

A solid record of performance supports the argument that operations will proceed more effectively with your having the latitude to make important decisions. With your direct connection with the issues in your job, you have the necessary understanding to respond quickly and accurately to the situation, adapting services to clients' needs or solving problems as they arise. This model is not only more effective, it's also quicker. The main challenge in your relationship with work is developing management's trust that you will make those decisions well as they arrive.

Build Control Through External Validation. Nothing impresses a boss or fellow team members more than happy clients. If you have a customer who gives good feedback about your performance on the job, you're much more likely to be given more control and authority over what you're doing. Similarly, if you win a prize for something, an award or any kind of recognition from a professional association or organization of your peers outside the company, everyone at the office will likely be darned impressed and give you a whole lot more respect, hence control over your own direction and destiny.

See Table 5.1, which illustrates an action plan for implementing the objectives discussed in this section.

Table 5.1. Action Progress Form

Area of Work Life: Control
Problem: Micromanagement

The Objective	The Target	Actions	Time Line	Progress
1. Increasing autonomy	Micromanage back.	• Identify opportunities. • Clarify your priorities and schedules. • Structure information in detail.	• 3 weeks • 2 weeks • 2 weeks	• • •
2. Increasing autonomy	Push the limits.	• Identify opportunities. • Set modest initial objectives. • Take action to extend authority.	• 2 weeks • 2 weeks • 4 weeks	• • •
3. Increasing autonomy	Build control with performance.	• Review accomplishments. • Construct persuasive arguments. • Meet with supervisor.	• 2 months • 1 month • 1 month	• • •
4. Increasing autonomy	Build control through external validation.	• Increase involvement in professional organizations. • Take on decision-making responsibilities. • Build reputation.	• 6 months • 1 year • 1 year	• • •

Control Objective: Shared Leadership

Here are some strategies for taking action to share leadership with a weak or ineffective supervisor.

Take Creative Control. Creative control includes the actions that initiate new projects. Without someone taking a lead role on initiating, you can get stuck in familiar routines, so you have no freedom to try something new. This is a serious control issue for you as an individual, as a record of innovation is key to advancement in most careers in the twenty-first century. Another dimension of creative control is brainstorming and other procedures for developing new concepts or processes. It may be that your boss is completely neglecting innovation in your department or that you are being left out of whatever creative innovation that is happening. In either case, it's up to you to bring that quality to your work life.

The first step is preparation. You think through your work, looking for creative openings. Once you find an idea you like, take the initiative on developing a concept. When meeting with your boss, introduce the project as part of your work plan, establishing it as a legitimate part of your responsibilities. This is an important step, as new ideas often need new funding. The first time your boss hears about the idea should not be when you're asking for money.

Take Critical Control. An essential leadership function is ensuring high standards of quality and performance. These functions are fundamental to building a reputation for excellence as an organization or as an individual. When this form of leadership is lacking, you are not pushed to do your best. You notice the organization tolerating shoddy work from colleagues.

Taking critical control requires a delicate touch. If your actions amount only to critiquing your colleagues' work, you could come across as competitive and unsupportive. A more acceptable approach is to begin critiquing your own work. You can review this critique with your supervisor, asking for additional advice on ways to improve the work. Even if your supervisor has nothing useful to add, you've introduced critical evaluation into your discussions. From this point, you can shift the focus to the work of other individuals or groups within the department.

Take Supportive Control. Another dimension of leadership is being supportive. Through encouraging words, attention to accomplishments, celebrations of success, and sympathy under duress, a leader provides emotional support to the individuals in the department. When these interactions are lacking in your relationship with your supervisor, it's hard to know where you stand: Is your supervisor taking your accomplishments or strains for granted, or is your supervisor just emotionally flat?

You can take control of this dimension of the relationship by providing these functions for your supervisor. In your discussions, express sympathy for your boss's difficulties and congratulations for accomplishments. It just might rub off. If not, you're developing a leadership style that will be appreciated.

See Table 5.2, which illustrates an action plan for implementing the objectives discussed in this section.

Control Objective: Team Rehab

Practice family therapy with your team, but never call it that. Once you've identified where the dysfunction might be, consider these strategies.

Communicate. The enabling condition for team decisions is communication. When they get together, the team needs to be talking about important issues. An effective team has a capacity to talk openly about important ideas. Members can express contrasting opinions without being bogged down in conflict or defensiveness.

Any occasion that brings together team members is an opportunity for communication. Identify a few issues of importance to the group. Rather than simply mulling them over on your own or having

Table 5.2. Action Progress Form

Area of Work Life: Control
Problem: Ineffective Leadership

The Objective	The Target	Actions	Time Line	Progress
1. Shared leadership	Take creative control.	• Identify opportunities. • Explore innovative ideas. • Inform supervisor. • Initiate pilot project.	• 3 weeks • 2 weeks • 2 weeks • 2 weeks	• • • •
2. Shared leadership	Take critical control.	• Identify opportunities. • Critique your own work. • Broaden focus of critique.	• 2 weeks • 2 weeks • 4 weeks	• • •
3. Shared leadership	Take supportive control.	• Identify opportunities. • Express support to colleagues. • Express support to your boss.	• 2 weeks • 2 weeks • 4 weeks	• • •

a one-on-one conversation with a colleague, introduce the topic to the group. Encourage people to express their views. Be supportive of people who express unpopular opinions. The point of this activity is not making momentous decisions; it's just to get people talking.

Focus.   A team with a good communication culture becomes more effective through making decisions together. The challenge at this point is finding ways of putting decisions in front of the group. Although achieving consensus on a selection of pizza toppings could serve as a step along the way, progress is quicker with more substantial issues under discussion.

A direct approach is to just start talking. Begin by talking about the topic under discussion and end by talking about the more substantial issue that is requiring the group's attention. It may be that the group's desire to discuss the issue will outweigh the leader's efforts to get the discussion back within the confines of the agenda. A thorough discussion of an important issue is a step toward group decision-making processes that would enhance the group's control over important aspects of the members' work life.

Review Tasks.   Problem-solving sessions to improve the team's operations are an effective place to start regaining control of your work life. It is what the team knows best, and it's the area that management is most likely to leave to the team's discretion. If this kind of problem solving is not a regular part of the team's operations, then your challenge is to find a way to get it started.

One entry point is to review a specific task, like launching your company's design for next season's line of gray flannel suits. When a team takes on a new operation or one of its usual operations is larger or more complex than usual, it's an opportunity to reflect, to consider what went right and what could go better next time. To control the transition, the group needs to build a shared understanding of what it is doing. Otherwise it could lose control of its primary agenda, with individual team members working at cross-purposes.

The first issue is how to get the conversation going. In the formal meeting format, you work through the team leader. One approach is to suggest the discussion prior to the meeting, seeking to introduce the new design into the agenda. This approach works with a team leader who is open to suggestions on shaping the meeting agenda. If that's not the case, it may work better to make the suggestion in the meeting.

The second issue is keeping the discussion positive. Reviewing a complex operation has the risk of individuals blaming one another for lapses in performance. This isn't going to help build team effectiveness or promote team decision making as a good idea. In choosing this strategy, a point to consider is whether you, or the team in general, can keep the discussion supportive rather than blaming.

Working as a more effective team member inspires others to do the same. You can do a lot by modeling effective team action. You can do more by actively recruiting team members to share your project.

See Table 5.3, which illustrates an action plan for implementing the objectives discussed in this section.

General Guidelines

Consider the following guidelines for solving workload problems.

Anticipate Resistance to Change

Power structures are highly resistant to change. People go to a lot of trouble to gain power; they don't relinquish it lightly. Changing the distribution of authority in an organization is a big job. The following list describes common forms of resistance to change that you are likely to encounter. The basic theme is that your attempts to increase your control can run into strategies that others have developed to increase or at least maintain their range of control.

- When attempting to push the limits, you may find the limits to be firm and tightly monitored. Having made a decision just

Table 5.3. Action Progress Form

Area of Work Life: Control
Problem: Ineffective Teams

The Objective	The Target	Actions	Time Line	Progress
1. Team rehab	Communicate.	• Identify neglected issues. • Encourage open conversations. • Initiate meeting discussions.	• 3 weeks • 2 weeks • 2 weeks	• • •
2. Team rehab	Focus.	• Identify potential decisions. • Influence meeting agendas. • Promote discussions.	• 2 weeks • 2 weeks • 4 weeks	• • •
3. Team rehab	Review tasks.	• Identify task for focus. • Initiate discussion. • Maintain constructive focus.	• 2 weeks • 2 weeks • 2 weeks	• • •

outside your usual range of operation, you may receive a phone call. Or your supervisor may casually mention in passing that your request for authorization seems to have been delayed. These are signs of the system reasserting itself in the face of your initiatives toward change.

- You may be seeking much more substantial reallocations of authority than are available through subtle interventions. You may have to change your job or even your profession to obtain a radical expansion of your authority. Unless you elect to revamp your career, steady increments in your authority, your capacity to work with a team, and your exercise leadership functions may be what are available in the immediate future.

- Your supervisor or team leader may jealously guard leadership prerogatives, even the ones being neglected. The leader may respond to your initiatives by addressing the gap. The reaction may be only short-lived, serving only to protect the status quo rather than signaling a shift in leadership behavior.

- Your team members may not share your enthusiasm for communication and decision making. Your communication initiatives may just fall flat. The agenda items may languish without discussion. Leading a team to effective action is not an instant process. Team building works more readily with a keen sensitivity to the group's readiness to enhance its level of operation.

Build Alliances

Your colleagues at work likely share many of your concerns. They may be having their own problems with control in your organization. They also will have a good idea of your capabilities. They can support your arguments for a greater level of professional responsibilities. They can also provide useful advice if you appear to be overreaching yourself. For example, Betty, the emergency room nurse discussed in Chapter Four, asked a good friend on the unit to let her know if the head nurse ever gave any signs of being perturbed or upset by the scheduling interventions.

The following list outlines points to consider in building alliances. It's important to consider that alliances can be limited to a single focus, such as enhancing team decision making. An alliance can be focused on one clear purpose for a limited time.

- You can find yourself subject to criticism when you take on greater responsibilities at work. By approaching the challenge as a team effort, you have defined a support group. The cooperation of others defines your initiative as more of a group effort. It's not simply an individual power trip, but a way for people to work together more effectively.

- You could enhance the impact of your initiatives to introduce leadership functions into your relationship with your supervisor by encouraging a colleague to do likewise with the same supervisor.

- Improving team effectiveness and leadership are more readily suited to a group undertaking. Trying to do these things on your own is a bit odd. The solution doesn't fit the problem.

Assess Your Risks

Attempting to increase your control has its risks. Any bid for increased power or for reducing the power that others have over your work may be interpreted as threatening. You are vulnerable to criticism from colleagues or managers who could depict your efforts to increase your autonomy as a refusal to be a team player. For example, the marketing manager of a major pet food distributor made a case to the executive responsible for his district to assign responsibility for a major advertising campaign. The executive, who hoped to use his leadership of this campaign as a means for advancement, interpreted the request as a power grab from the manager and turned it down flat.

The following list sets out some of the common risks that you may encounter when attempting to enhance control in your work life. Your initiatives occur in a social context, requiring close attention to others who may well have their own concerns about control in their work lives.

- It pays to bring other people on your side with your plans to increase autonomy. Let others know your intentions. Your efforts will be more acceptable to others if you communicate consistently your willingness to cooperate with others on shared concerns. For example, a shared leadership initiative undertaken as a group builds a group's capacity to work together, whereas unilaterally changing your mode of interaction with the group could isolate you from the group.

- With greater autonomy comes greater responsibility. Even though you can confidently take greater credit for your successes, others will also blame you for more problems. Increased autonomy brings with it an obligation to think through the potential consequences of actions. This may be a difficult challenge. Although you may have greater freedom in some areas of your work, you will not be able to make events unfold consistently according to your plans.

- Be careful to avoid overstating your authority. Both colleagues and supervisors are likely to take offense.

- Be ready to relinquish a leadership role to your supervisor. The point of the intervention is to enhance the quality of the leadership relationship, not to preempt your boss's job.

Step Four: Tracking Progress

The first thing to assess is whether you actually implemented the components of your plan. In the final column of the Action Progress Form, note the date at which each component of the plan is implemented. For components that take more than one day to implement, note the beginning and ending dates.

An Illustrative Story

Matilda is looking for greater control in her work as an interior designer. In our previous contact with Matilda, her design for the local branch of a financial planning firm had been blocked by Rodney.

Rodney recognizes that Matilda has developed a clever design but dismisses it as too expensive and trendy for a client whose driving value is cost containment. Rodney's position as department head gives him the authority to overrule Matilda. She is deeply offended by his dismissive judgment and angry about his exercise of authority over her professional expertise.

Matilda is looking for a relationship in which she is recognized as an equal partner based on her professional expertise. A relationship in which people of lesser professional expertise have control over her work and can overrule her judgment is a serious mismatch. She experiences a mismatch between the freedom required to work according to her professional aspirations and the constraints imposed by Rodney's management authority.

A lack of control has implications for other strategic areas. Matilda has increased her workload by devoting time and energy beyond working hours to developing a design that will go nowhere. She lost the opportunity to be rewarded when her design was vetoed. She feels unfairly treated by Rodney, because of his unilateral exercise of power over the group's design. Most important, Matilda's lack of control prevents her from fulfilling her values through her profession. This mismatch pits Matilda's professional values, her enjoyment of creative design work, and her independent spirit against Rodney's commitment to cost containment, backed by his power to block developments that conflict with his values. And in this confrontation, Rodney's values dominate.

Following the Four Steps

Here's how Matilda worked the four steps.

Step One: Defining the Problem: Being Micromanaged

Matilda's initial diagnosis of her problem was that her work life was dominated by a blithering, micromanaging idiot.

Indications in the My Relationship with Work Test. Karen scored major mismatches on C4, C5, C6, C7, C8, C9, and C10. All of these items pertain to her level of autonomy relative to the management structure of the company.

Step Two: Setting Objectives: Increasing Autonomy

Matilda was determined to increase her professional autonomy. She wanted greater influence over the design decisions. She was happy to work with the design team to make these decisions, but she did not accept that an individual could overrule her professional judgment on the basis of holding a middle management position.

Step Three: Taking Action: Building Control Through External Validation

Resolution of a mismatch can work on either end of the imbalance. Focusing on Rodney and the larger organizational context, Matilda considered changing Rodney's values so that he would have an appreciation for the elegance of her design as well as his already deep commitment to cost containment. Matilda imagined how—through a concerted, subtle, and persistent campaign—she could educate and influence Rodney to appreciate the power of her more elegant designs to meet the needs of clients who may believe at first that their only consideration is cost containment. Matilda rejected this idea because she did not see enough evidence of Rodney's aesthetic sensibilities to warrant the effort.

Matilda considered changing her expectations for the job. As a designer—especially one fairly early in her career—Matilda needed a base. She needed to work with an organization to gain experience, to make contacts, and to learn the practical dimensions of design work. Although her long-term goal was establishing her independent approach to design, it may have been that the time to do that had not yet arrived. This may be the point in her career for attending to the established way of doing things. Matilda acknowledged that there was something to be said for being a good corporate citizen, doing what management requested, and doing it well. But she rejected this idea because she was too young and idealistic to relinquish her professional values. She'd rather go back to the cocktail waitress job that had gotten her through design school.

Matilda chose to change the balance of power through her professional associations. She worked on building her external prestige to enhance her power base within the organization. She became an active member of the state interior design association and contributed to their programs. She figured that with sufficient fame and a capacity to draw clients seeking her personal involvement in developing their designs, a manager would be hesitant to overrule any of her designs.

Matilda submitted the rejected design to the regional competition that was conducted by the state interior design association. She received second prize for a commercial space development concept and a lot of media attention. In the following weeks, a few clients asked specifically for Matilda when contacting the firm for work. Rodney, who could determine quickly which way the wind was blowing, gave Matilda a lot more control. He mentioned to his boss how he'd always been impressed by the obvious talent in that young woman.

Step Four: Tracking Progress

A year later, Matilda reviewed her task list for building external credibility and gave high marks to herself for each step of the process. Her colleagues saw her success as reflecting well on the team, giving them a new sense of effectiveness as a group. Her My Relationship with Work Test items continued to have a few mismatches, but the major mismatches were gone.

Chapter Six

Solving Reward Problems

A mismatch on reward means a lack of motivation, gratification, fulfillment, appreciation, self-worth, self-esteem, even love. Something is missing. This activity—your job, your career—that consumes a huge amount of your time, energy, and talent feels empty. The returns are not worth your effort. What's the point? This is serious.

Step One: Defining the Problem

The My Relationship with Work Test helps pin down the qualities of your work life that are less than fulfilling. When all the *reward* items are mismatches, you are in a very difficult situation that is hard to sustain. When the mismatches are focused within a limited range of potential rewards, the problem becomes more manageable.

Reward Problem: Insufficient Compensation

Money is always an issue. There never seems to be enough. But it becomes a major mismatch when inadequate pay causes a hardship, a continuing sense of rage, anxiety, and depression. It is also a mismatch when you're aware that others in similar positions are being compensated more handsomely.

Indications in the My Relationship with Work Test. Insufficient compensation is noted by mismatches on R1, R2, R6, R7, and R8. These items pertain to money and benefits.

Reward Problem: Lack of Recognition

Regardless of whether the pay is adequate, you like your work to be appreciated. Money is not the only barometer of this kind of feedback. Organizations and groups have other ways to express appreciation, respect, and compensation. They may present regular awards, for example, in the form of certificates, plaques, or small presents. They may grant certain employees special perks, privileges, trips, extra vacation days. There are a broad variety of ways that a group or company may let its employees know something that is very important: we appreciate what you're doing, we like you, we want you to enjoy some special form of recognition.

You want key people to notice your contribution and react positively if not enthusiastically. There is an emptiness when recognition is missing.

Indications in the My Relationship with Work Test. Lack of recognition is indicated by mismatches on R3, R4, and R7.

Reward Problem: Unsatisfying Work

If you're not in it for the money or the glory, then the work ought to be enjoyable. Many jobs give people the opportunity to develop highly refined skills that are well suited to their abilities. Opportunities to exercise those skills and to develop them further are highly fulfilling. Being deprived of those opportunities to be stuck in tedium is a major disappointment.

Indications in the My Relationship with Work Test. Unsatisfying work is indicated by mismatches on R9 and R10.

Step Two: Setting Objectives

The objectives in this section are aimed at making work life more rewarding. They aim to build rewards where they are lacking or improve their quality where they are in short supply. All of the objectives require changing people or processes at work.

Reward Objective for Insufficient Compensation: More Money

Money appears simple at first glance, but there are distinct dimensions to inadequate pay. Most large organizations have detailed compensation policies that spell out the pay for the various positions. Your objective may be to improve your salary by bringing it in line with policy, or you may intend to go beyond what is designated by business as usual. The difference between these two objectives can lead to distinct strategies.

Money may also take equivalent forms, beyond actual cash, such as additional perks, like better offices, parking places, or an expense account. In many instances when an actual increase in compensation is resisted or deferred, these kinds of perks may fill the gap, if properly negotiated and applied. Benefits that go beyond straight salary to incentive programs, variable pay based on performance goals, special health and life insurance, special tuition payments for family members—these are other elements in a compensation package that can be a factor in your overall reward on the job. And if you're fortunate to be in a position where stock options are available, this too can be extremely important in terms of long-term compensation.

Reward Objective for Lack of Recognition: Acknowledgment

Recognition of accomplishments comes in different forms. Some are more meaningful than others. In some organizations, annual employee prizes and recognition awards can be a coveted distinction, given to truly innovative employees; in other organizations, it simply identifies who's in good with the boss this week.

On a more day-to-day level, some supervisors readily wax eloquent about employees' accomplishments; others give little evidence that they're aware of who is doing what. Gaining recognition in the latter case requires bringing about a significant change in personal style.

Reward Objective for Unsatisfying Work: Better Job Assignments

Improving your work assignments is a reward that has a major impact on your day-to-day work life. Payday comes every few weeks; a smile from your supervisor may be a rare event. But you're doing your work all day, every day. And it's the intrinsic satisfaction of doing enjoyable work that stays with you.

The point of improving your job assignments is to increase the proportion of your time at work that you can devote to activities that you enjoy. Often these are activities that you perceive to be making a positive contribution to the quality of the company's work and to the satisfaction of its customers. But in some cases, it is simply the activity: writing the report, analyzing the stock portfolio, caring for the statue, or tuning the piano, that you enjoy, regardless of its impact or anyone's appreciation.

Step Three: Taking Action

Improving your level of rewards can be a concerted campaign over an extended period. Some rewards are in short supply. Other rewards require new skills or attitudes on the part of key people in your work life. Still others require thinking through new ways of organizing work across the organization. Although a few quick wins are possible, progress often calls for a concerted campaign.

Reward Objective: More Money

Increasing our paychecks is a subject dear to the hearts of millions. There are many books and Web sites devoted to asking for a raise. This can be a multiyear campaign or a one-day wonder. It can be a fascinating interaction touching on issues of your value to the organization and the reciprocal nature of your working relationship. Or it can just be a hard-knuckle bargaining session about money. And in such a confrontation, it's crucial that you present yourself as a valuable asset to the company in general and to your supervisor in particular.

Negotiating a Raise. Negotiating a raise is a persuasive communication of enormous consequence. As with other negotiations in your work life, a successful outcome requires careful preparation. Solid arguments must be based on empirical data with no exaggeration. It's important to present the argument in a compelling fashion and to respect the perspective of the audience.

One of the solid arguments for a raise is *equity:* you are looking for compensation that is comparable to that of other people in the company or in comparable positions in other companies. A contrasting argument is for *distinction:* you should receive more than the modest salary of others in comparable positions because you are extraordinarily gifted. Both sorts of arguments have been successful, but only when there is a good fit with the situation.

A compelling argument is tightly structured, conveyed succinctly, and well timed. It helps to outline your arguments to ensure that you don't drop important points. The discussion may be a bit stressful, leading you to neglect some key points. Succinctness is important. Managers prefer discussions that are crisp and to the point. Fitting into that value increases your credibility. There are certain times in the course of the year or the quarter when adjusting a salary may be more likely. It does not help to deliver a compelling argument for a raise six months before your boss has the prescribed ability to take action.

Giving an Ultimatum. An ultimatum takes the discussion to another level of intensity. As noted earlier, an ultimatum is not to be delivered lightly. Your boss may not have the power or inclination to meet your demands, leaving you to seek other employment opportunities.

In some circumstances, an ultimatum may be appropriate. Some organizations only address salary demands when an employee has a firm offer from elsewhere. If that is your organizational culture and you are a highly valued employee, and you can secure an alternative job offer, this may be the way to go. And along the way, you may decide that the other job offer actually looks like an attractive possibility.

Reducing Output. The other side of the equity balance is your contribution. That is, if the organization is not rewarding you sufficiently for your contribution, you could diminish your contribution. It has been proposed that people actually react in this way without necessarily intending to. There is a compelling tendency in relationships to balance things out. When we're given much, we tend to give much in return. When the other party in a relationship is stingy, we tend to respond likewise.

Finding Other Sources of Income. Another way to approach the problem of inadequate reward is to seek other work on a freelance or part-time basis. This both increases your total income and provides some independence, perspective, and leverage for ultimately leaving altogether. This option requires that you have the time, energy, and contacts to find opportunities. It also assumes that your current employment does not forbid you from doing extra work.

The process of establishing yourself as a freelance worker is a self-promotion campaign. The preparation is putting together presentations and written material that describe your talents and the benefits of your services. You develop a profile through your external contacts. You can bypass this step when an opportunity approaches you in the course of your regular work. A firm that is familiar with your work may inquire about your availability to work on a designated project. This initial work could be the first of a sequence of opportunities.

A simpler route is finding a part-time job to supplement your current employment. You're saved the hassles of promoting your services and comprehending new tax forms. And your efforts can go directly to your objective by providing more money.

See Table 6.1, which illustrates an action plan for implementing the objectives discussed in this section.

Table 6.1. Action Progress Form

Area of Work Life: Reward
Problem: Insufficient Compensation

The Objective	The Target	Actions	Time Line	Progress
1. More money	Negotiating a raise	• Develop equity or recognition arguments. • Choose optimal time. • Meet with boss.	• 3 weeks • ? • 2 weeks	• • •
2. More money	Giving an ultimatum	• Consider implications. • Consider employment alternatives. • Meet with boss.	• 2 weeks • 2 weeks • 4 weeks	• • •
3. More money	Reducing output	• Review current productivity. • Identify potential areas for reducing contribution. • Adjust contribution.	• 1 month • 1 month • 1 month	• • •
4. More money	Finding other sources of income	• Investigate opportunities. • Build ongoing opportunities.	• 6 months • 1 year	• •

Reward Objective: Acknowledgment

You're doing great things at work, but is anyone noticing? Recognition from key people in the organization feels good. It builds you up and confirms that you're on the right track. It may also be important for future opportunities. The key people will think of you as a going concern in the company. It's worth some effort to make it easy for people to recognize your accomplishments.

Training Your Supervisor. A principal focus of your activities in building a more fulfilling work life is your immediate supervisor. In many work situations, this is just one person. But it may be two people or more: you may participate in a variety of teams or have a reporting structure in which you answer to different people for various aspects of your work. Or it may be that your principal focus is not so much your immediate supervisor, but a manager a step or two up the line.

- Talk about the situation with your supervisor. Indicate your desire to contribute to the organization, referring specifically to contributing to the supervisor's unit. Indicate that it is important to you that your supervisor evaluate your daily work. This feedback lets you know when you're on the right track and motivates you to further efforts. Indicate that you'll do your part by keeping the supervisor informed of work in progress, during which time you hope for feedback; ask how the supervisor prefers to receive this information.
- Identify an accomplishment that is a clear success. Consider your accomplishments from your supervisor's point of view. It's not enough that you consider this accomplishment as a success; it must be something that your supervisor will consider a success. It doesn't just make you look good: it makes your supervisor and your unit look good by furthering the unit's objectives.
- Bring the matter to your supervisor's attention. Consider the best way to communicate an accomplishment to your supervi-

sor. For example, e-mail is easy to use, but your supervisor may be so overloaded with e-mails that your message gets lost.

Rewarding Yourself. While you're embarking on what may be a long period of training your supervisors, you need to keep your spirits high.

- Keep track of your major accomplishments and celebrate them. Reward yourself in a personal or private way that you really enjoy when you think you deserve it.
- Tell your colleagues, friends, and family when you feel good about something you've accomplished at work. Do rewarding events with others. Don't just eat a pint of ice cream all alone; go out with people whose company you enjoy. Along the way, note something significant that you accomplished in your work.

Acknowledging Others. The lack of rewards in your life may reflect a larger culture that neglects to acknowledge success. You can have an impact by modeling another approach. If it fills a need for others, it's likely to catch on.

- Keep track of your coworkers' accomplishments and celebrate them. Consider carefully how they would enjoy being acknowledged. If such interactions are rare, you might want to be fairly low-key.
- Look for opportunities to celebrate accomplishments of your work team: meeting a deadline or making it through a rush period, such as the holiday shopping season or registration week at a college. The emphasis of the celebration should be on excellent performance rather than on we're-so-glad-that's-over for another year.

See Table 6.2, which illustrates an action plan for implementing the objectives discussed in this section.

Table 6.2. Action Progress Form

Area of Work Life: Reward
Problem: Insufficient Recognition

The Objective	The Target	Actions	Time Line	Progress
1. Acknowledgment	Training your boss	• Develop arguments. • Meet with your boss. • Communicate accomplishments.	• 3 weeks • 2 weeks • 1 year	• • •
2. Acknowledgment	Rewarding yourself	• Track accomplishments. • Share with colleagues. • Celebrate.	• 3 months • 2 weeks • 4 weeks	• • •
3. Acknowledgment	Acknowledging others	• Track coworkers' accomplishments. • Celebrate shared accomplishments.	• 3 months • 1 month	• •

Reward Objective: Better Job Assignments

The objective of better job assignments is to find a sense of reward in spending more time doing what you enjoy. This objective involves influencing how work is organized within your department or team. It requires identifying the opportunities for doing more engaging work and how this shift in job responsibilities fits into the work group.

Negotiate Better Assignments.   Your primary argument in this negotiation with your supervisor or team is that the company gets a better value when you're doing work you enjoy. And your enjoyment inspires you to produce work of ever higher quality. This argument works best with companies that are committed to high-quality services or excellent craftsmanship in their products.

The challenges in the negotiation occur if most employees in the company prefer the same kind of work you enjoy, so competition is keen. The argument is not one of pure quality at this point, but it's that because of your skills, commitment, or long history with the company, you deserve preferential treatment. Another challenge for your supervisor is assigning the drudgery. If it's necessary work, someone besides you has to do it. That's a problem that a fully persuasive argument will address.

Expand and Increase What You Enjoy.   There may be some aspect of your current work that is more exciting than another. And there may be a way to focus more on those activities while at the same time cutting back on the drudgery. For example, Margaret, a college professor of English, despaired of the amount of work time that was devoted to marking first-year compositions. She greatly preferred devoting her time to writing scholarly articles on the poetry of John Donne.

While juggling the work of multiple sections of first-year composition, Margaret managed to write a brilliant proposal for a large national research grant. She included in that grant proposal funds for the English department to employ a part-time instructor to teach one of her courses each term, specifically freshman composition. She argued that this reduction in her teaching was the only way that she would have time to do the necessary research under the grant. The proposal, including the teaching reduction, was successful. Margaret had a more agreeable balance of work demands.

Change How to Do the Job. The problem may be the way the job is usually done rather than the job itself. If your job gives you a fair amount of latitude in how you get the job done, you can invent a new approach. You could develop something that makes better use of your skills, including more of the activities you enjoy in your work.

For example, Ken, a gregarious sales manager, regularly suffered through a few days every quarter when he put together the sales report for his division. He could do the work; he just preferred meeting with clients or having strategy sessions with his team. He hated spending days at a time behind a closed door alone, cranking out the text of the report.

It occurred to him one day to generate the report as a team project rather than as a solo job. He called the team together in a room with a computer projector. They all had a delightful time. And the report was finished in less time.

See Table 6.3, which illustrates an action plan for implementing the objectives discussed in this section.

General Guidelines

Here are some general guidelines to consider when embarking on action plans to make your work life more fulfilling. The general theme is that these changes occur in a social context in which people are aware of one another's rewards. One small change can have extensive reverberations.

Anticipate Resistance to Change

Some organizational cultures place a low priority on employees enjoying their work. Work is work; find your enjoyment elsewhere.

Table 6.3. Action Progress Form

Area of Work Life: Reward
Problem: Unsatisfying Work

The Objective	The Target	Actions	Time Line	Progress
1. Better job assignments	Negotiate better assignments.	• Develop arguments. • Meet with your boss. • Adjust work distribution.	• 3 weeks • 2 weeks • 1 year	• • •
2. Better job assignments	Increase what you enjoy.	• Track work distribution. • Excel at enjoyed tasks. • Adjust work distribution.	• 3 months • 1 year • 1 year	• • •
3. Better job assignments	Change how to do the job.	• Assess task procedures. • Develop alternative procedures. • Implement alternative procedures.	• 3 months • 1 year • 1 year	• • •

When enjoyment is recognized as an important dimension, there may be intense competition for scarce rewards.

The following are some points at which you may encounter resistance in your efforts to develop a more rewarding work life. One theme in this list is that organizations develop, over time, systems that slow down the extent to which it can respond to individual efforts to increase their balance of rewards. Another theme is that some individuals in key positions may begrudge acknowledging the accomplishments of others.

- Salary policies can seriously cramp your potential to negotiate a better deal financially. Unionized environments are especially rigid, having firm contractual obligations regarding salary and benefits.

- Many supervisors have a difficult time acknowledging their employees' successes. Even if they agree with you in principle that acknowledging successes is a good thing to do, it may not be in their repertoire. Your training program for your supervisor may be a long project.

- It can take a long time to learn to enjoy a new task. And some work activities may just be plain boring however you approach them.

Build Alliances

Your success will improve with alliances. People care about one another's level of reward. The more that you can build the support of other people for any of these initiatives, the more likely they are to succeed and endure.

As the following list indicates, improving your rewards need not be a winner-take-all game. There are ways in which collaborating with others increases the chances for your personal success.

- A review of salary policies across the work group could be a shared undertaking if equity is the primary issue. A serious consideration of compensation inequities could improve the situation for you and others as well.

- A team approach will accelerate building a supportive culture that recognizes the accomplishments of individuals and groups.
- Many dull tasks can be more enjoyable as a group project rather than as a solitary activity.

Assess Your Risks

Increasing rewards does not appear risky at first glance, but there are potential downsides. As indicated in the following list, others—individually or corporately—may take a dim view of your efforts to improve your lot in work life. What began as attempts to make your life more pleasant can instead fill it with conflict and risk.

- Attempting to improve your compensation relative to that of your colleagues could spark resentment.
- Managers could perceive your request for recognizing your accomplishments as indicating a lack of resilience, suggesting that you are excessively dependent on the approval of others.
- Your attempts to negotiate better task assignments may prompt greater competition from your colleagues for the same assignments.
- Taking outside employment may be perceived as a conflict of interest by your employer. It is important to check company policy and precedent thoroughly on this question.

Step Four: Tracking Progress

In some situations, your progress may be obvious. But sometimes you have to look closely to assess progress. And sometimes you need an accurate record to remember how different things used to be.

Are things improving? Along the way, it is useful to record your implementation of the action plan and reactions of clients, coworkers, managers, and the company in general to your initiatives.

In the final column of the Action Progress Form, note the dates on which you implemented each of the steps.

An Illustrative Story

Elaine was a freelance writer with a graduate degree in clinical psychology. She wrote articles for a variety of publications on the process, strains, and joys of decision making. She had created a business opportunity for herself, free from the humdrum hassles of corporate life, after resigning from her position as a researcher at a university.

When she began freelancing, there was a steady flow of interesting work. Her reputation, built on a few key research findings, had marketed her services. The work came to her with no effort on her part. All she had to do was write. That's what she likes to do and that is what she does well. And she was making good money, much better than in her old job. Things were just perfect.

After two years, however, her business model stopped working. The assignments that came to her were dull and uninspiring. Over and again, she had to find something fresh, humorous, and—yes—uplifting to say about the process of shopping for purses. Or shoes. Magazine editors liked articles on shopping; they kept the advertisers happy. The writing paid the bills, but it didn't do much more than pay the bills. She had little opportunity to put anything new or unique into these assignments. The work got dull quickly, and she lost her reputation for cutting-edge perspectives.

Following the Four Steps

Here's how Elaine worked the four steps.

Step One: Defining the Problem: Insufficient Compensation

Elaine was bored and broke. Her work assignments had become much duller and less lucrative. After her initial success faded, she was making less money than in her previous job. She had more expenses and no employer-provided benefits.

Indications in the My Relationship with Work Test. Elaine scored mismatches on many items, starting with R1 and R2 as major mismatches, as the work was no longer paying the bills. She scored major mismatches on R9 and R10, reflecting the dull writing assignments.

Step Two: Setting Objectives: More Money

Elaine set as an objective to arrange better-paying job assignments. She had begun to doubt whether the freelance life was the life for her, but she felt she had to give it her best shot. Her objective went beyond making the assignments just a bit more interesting. She was determined to get assignments that would go beyond those that she was doing when she first went independent. So she began to speculate about the decision-making process in selecting partners in relationships and ultimately how people decided to get married.

Step Three: Taking Action: Negotiating Better Assignments

Elaine's ultimate strategy was to reinvent herself as a relationship guru: a serious psychologist who could advise men and women on the crucial decisions of their relationships and their personal lives. A kind of Dr. Joyce Brothers for the twenty-first century. Improving her work assignments meant marketing her writing to magazine editors across the city, attending trade shows, and renewing her contract with a publicist to get some air time on TV and radio to revitalize her profile. She had to reassert her position as someone with a fresh perspective. That required her to do extensive research on new developments in decision-making research and modern relationships. She had a talent for translating obscure research findings into plain English. That talent was what got her established as a writer originally, but she had not been attending to innovations. The whole action plan was thorough, although expensive and time-consuming.

It worked, but it took a year to get things back to where they were when she first set up as a freelance writer. And she really enjoyed the new writing assignments, as well as the notoriety her efforts brought. And the money was much better.

Step Four: Tracking Progress

After a year, Elaine no longer had major mismatches on reward. Her scores on R1, R2, R9, and R10 were a match. But she was feeling the effect of the workload and had gained a respect for the work of the marketing staff. She was confirmed in her intention to work independently, but she appreciated how much planning and hard work were required to stay on top of the game.

Chapter Seven

Solving Community Problems

Every workplace is a community of men and women who spend a whole lot of time together. Figure it out: the hours, days, weeks, years. In many case, you'll find that you're spending more time at your workplace community than you are at home with your family and friends.

All of us who've spent a lot of time at work know this and know that every workplace has a unique and distinct atmosphere, a culture that permeates the environment from top to bottom and in every nook and cranny. Some workplace communities are very stable, relatively pleasant, and productive. But if you have major mismatches in the area of community on the My Relationship with Work Test, then you may be working in a community that has big problems, one that is dysfunctional, oppressive, mean-spirited, abusive even, precipitating your burnout, and making you miserable.

When the social environment of work does not coalesce into a happy and functional community, all sorts of things go wrong. People can be too much with you, overwhelming you with their demands, distractions, or diversions. Colleagues can be absent, distant, or cold, leaving you lonely and isolated. Fellow workers can be actively unpleasant to the point of abuse, rude to the point of offense, or unresponsive to the point of indifference.

Losing the opportunity to participate in a functional and supportive workplace community is a serious mismatch at work. Relationships with people are fundamental to a productive, fulfilling work life. We learn and develop through supportive guidance from mentors. There is a joy in being part of a cohesive team that is addressing a shared challenge with enthusiasm. We may develop some of our closest friendships at work. Many people even find the love of their life at work. The community at work can and should be a comfortable social environment, populated by people you know and with whom you develop significant and ongoing relationships.

A major mismatch across the ten community items represents a serious career crisis and potential for major burnout. Your expectations and aspirations for social interaction at work are not being met. This could be a matter of style: your way of being with people isn't accepted or supported. It could be situational: you could be working with a particularly difficult group of people, who are nasty, intolerant, or cold. It could be a matter of skills: it may be difficult for you to take an active role in team discussions or keep up with the chatter over the course of the day at work. Regardless of the problem's source, the objective is to develop fulfilling, pleasant, and productive relationships with others at work.

Step One: Defining the Problem

If you have identified *community* as one of the workplace areas that is contributing to your burnout, it may be for specific idiosyncratic reasons that are unique to your organizational culture. Generally speaking, however, we've found that when problems exist in this area, they usually center on one of the following areas.

Community Problem: Divisiveness

A pervasive problem of organizations across the public and private sector is divisiveness. Individuals and groups in organizations can become divided into isolated or even hostile camps. There may be competition, fear, paranoia, and hostility among departments, between management and employees, between one branch of the office and another. Within their groups, individuals have nothing good to say about the other groups. Rather than participating in a community that spans the organization, employees have a sense of togetherness only with their subgroup. Their allegiance to their group actually inhibits developing a sense of community that spans the organization. It's a mean and nasty, adversarial, counterproductive situation that can totally destroy the cohesiveness, cooperation, and coordination that's necessary for any workplace community to function and for anyone who works there, such as you, to feel at all happy on the job.

Indications in the My Relationship with Work Test. Divisiveness is indicated by mismatches on S8, S9, and S10. (S is used to stand for *social work environment,* so as to distinguish this category from the C that is used in the control section.)

Community Problem: Poor Communication

A precondition for a sense of happy and functional community is an awareness of what is happening in the organization. You can't feel part of something if you don't know what's going on. Unfortunately, organizations that translate a suspicious culture into a policy of limited or poor communication often conduct business behind closed doors. They're secretive and mysterious. They create an atmosphere of ignorance, fear of the unknown, and speculation about potential harm and disaster. How can you know what to do if you don't have the necessary data, if there's no transparency, openness, and honesty about results, policies, goals? It's remarkable how many businesses and organizations actually behave this way.

Indications in the My Relationship with Work Test. Poor communication is indicated by mismatches on S1, S2, and S3.

Community Problem: Alienation

A vibrant and effective work community has a strong sense of mutual support and togetherness. Individuals sympathize with one another's frustrations and celebrate their successes. An alienated social environment lacks human connection, empathy, and warmth. Interactions among coworkers serve only to get the job done and may not do that very well. Each individual feels alone, separate, not a part of the whole, and powerless.

Indications in the My Relationship with Work Test. Having no support is noted by mismatches on S4, S5, S6, and S7.

Step Two: Setting Objectives

By setting a few small but clear objectives, you can really begin to improve the atmosphere of the workplace community.

Community Objective for Divisiveness: Conflict Resolution

When your workplace is an armed camp of hostile groups, it's like a military or legal battleground. So the first thing you have to do is create an atmosphere where you can begin to identify and resolve the most obvious disputes.

Just the act of admitting that these disputes exist is a great beginning. Agreeing that the conflicts are a problem and beginning to identify what they are is a great leap forward toward a process of reconciliation.

Community Objective for Poor Communication: Better Communication

In the world of organizational psychology and human relationships, there is considerable expertise readily available on improving communication on any level: corporate, departmental, team, small group, or one-on-one. There really is no excuse for poor communication. Yes, it requires time, effort, and expertise to improve communication. But it's a core function of an organization, an essential element of getting the job done, whatever that job happens to be, and a critical part of everyone's public and private life.

So don't let anyone tell you that communication can't be improved. There are literally hundreds of books, training programs, videos, DVDs, and tapes on the topic, plus thousands of coaches who can come in and help you out.

Community Objective for Alienation: Unity

A strong feeling of connection, empathy for your fellow workers, mutual support, and common cause are all qualities that are most attractive about a good workplace community. People are fully capable of showing support for one another. The challenge is developing an organizational culture that values and nurtures supportive relationships.

Step Three: Taking Action

A sense of community at work is brought about through common goals, teamwork, mutual support, and learning together. These qualities make a practical contribution to your capacity to do your job. These are also enjoyable qualities of going to work. The working relationships that develop with colleagues through these activities are an enduring benefit of your work.

Community Objective: Conflict Resolution

As with communication (discussed later in the chapter), there is a lot of expertise on resolving disputes at work. We're all familiar with major intracompany disputes that had to be settled through union negotiations or in the courts. But we'd like to avoid those extreme measures and consider some other strategies that have been highly successful in improving community relationships where various factions and different parts of an organization have been at war with one another.

Find Common Ground. Organizational communities are by definition formed in the first place for shared goals: producing a service or product, in some cases making a profit, in all cases surviving on a financial level so they can continue to operate, and—of course —providing a workplace culture where people are happy and want to stay.

If you are having a major community problem in your workplace, you can emphasize the importance of the issue to your leadership, your management, your team members. If you're on some level of management yourself, emphasize the issue to your direct reports and employees. The message is, "We all have the same reason for being here; we're all in the same boat. If we don't pull together, we're going to sink." Repeat the message until *it* sinks in.

One excellent way to renew this sense of shared goals and common ground is to reorganize what may be a fragmented work process or create a new project that overlaps or spans across various departments and factions in an organization. A boundary-spanning project is one that pulls together individuals from the various divisions of the organization on a short-term basis. It can be anything from creating a new product (which could involve design, manufacturing, marketing, and sales) to targeting regional sales for improved results (involving financial analysis, sales, marketing, and branch offices).

Increase Civility. If you are suffering from burnout as a result of community problems, you must be suffering from day-to-day acrimony in the workplace, an atmosphere where people are impolite and rude to one another, say mean and abusive things to one another, and often use profanity and other insulting language.

It's quite possible to confront this with zero tolerance on an individual level. Such behavior can be dealt with one-to-one or can be referred to personnel, human resources, or management, as a matter of public law and company policy.

Beyond that, there are actually trainings and off-sites supervised by professionals who specialize in coaching and encouraging the benefits of civility.

Try Mediation. Some forms of divisiveness are so ingrained, nasty, and persistent that they appear entirely immune to gentle persuasion. A formal mediation process may be necessary to get the problem in the open as an issue requiring action for the good of the larger company.

Although individual employees can't single-handedly initiate a mediation process, they can encourage it. The following actions are steps that can encourage the organization to address divisiveness seriously:

- *Identify the issues.* Major conflicts within a large organization persist without being acknowledged as problems or as issues requiring action from senior management. You can make the issue salient by raising the topic in your conversations with managers. Suggestion boxes or formats for asking questions of the CEO provide another route to give official recognition to the problem.

- *Share case examples.* Research examples from other organizations that have tackled problems in divisiveness. Look for techniques that help groups span boundaries to make the organizational mission primary over divisional conflicts. There are actually lots of resources available for mediation and conflict resolution, many precedents, several professional organizations, and services that specialize in resolving such disputes. By sharing the results of this research, you go beyond identifying the issue to giving hope that the problem is amenable to action.

- *Participate.* If management does take any action to acknowledge or address the issue, participate. The process may begin with a few trial balloons to determine if anyone cares about the issue. Any contribution you can make to increase the momentum toward action moves you a bit closer to a constructive community at work.

See Table 7.1, which illustrates an action plan for implementing the objectives discussed in this section.

Table 7.1. Action Progress Form

Area of Work Life: Community
Problem: Divisiveness

The Objective	The Target	Actions	Time Line	Progress
1. Conflict resolution	Find common ground.	• Identify fragmented process. • Bring together stakeholders. • Identify alternative processes.	• 3 weeks • 1 month • 2 months	• • •
2. Conflict resolution	Increase civility.	• Respond firmly to rudeness. • Encourage civility training. • Participate in civility training.	• 3 months • 3 months • 3 months	• • •
3. Conflict resolution	Try mediation.	• Identify the issues. • Share examples of successful mediation. • Participate in mediation.	• 3 months • 1 year • 1 year	• • •

Community Objective: Better Communication

The following strategies are ways of building better communication.

Reach Out. Expand your own circles. Don't just stick with your little group, team, or segment of the organization. Even in an age of e-mail, cell phones, and global communication, it's all too easy to settle into a communication pattern with a limited number of contacts. You are most likely to communicate with people just nearby, whom you encounter in your daily movements around the office. These people are likely the ones in your department or subunit, especially those with whom you have a defined working relationship, such as supervision or coordination. These contacts are useful and necessary, but they're insufficient. They leave you with a limited set of contacts, determined more by geography than intention.

Instead make up a personal communication plan that includes a new roster of people whom you want to talk to, write to, and call. This can help you rise above the pattern of interactions that characterize your day-to-day work life. The plan is doubly important in social environments marked by divisiveness, as the plan provides one of the few qualities encouraging you toward communicating beyond your immediate group.

Listen to Messages. You may not be the only one with a constructive communication plan. There may be other individuals, groups, or departments that are striving actively to cross boundaries through a concerted communication campaign. In the contemporary workplace, it is tempting to dispose of e-mails, newsletters, and announcements with the most minimal glance. You can set e-mail filters that will prevent messages from specified groups or individuals from ever seeing the light of day in your in box. This is an essential function for controlling spam but could be a bit excessive when filtering messages from other parts of the organization.

You couldn't attend to every message every day, even if you didn't have a job to do. That's not a viable strategy. But you can review the pattern of messages from various quarters in the organization to identify those that are distributing constructive information that helps you appreciate the full scope of the organization beyond your immediate work context. In the time-pressured flow of your work, it may be necessary to schedule time on a regular basis to attend to messages from reliable sources of useful news and to scan the larger volume of messages to identify new sources worthy of your attention.

Ask Questions.   You can accelerate your strategy beyond attending to useful messages by challenging events and communications that reinforce divisiveness in the company. In a hostile, divided environment, a direct confrontation may only serve to perpetuate the divisions. A milder approach is generally more politic.

Ask questions. Nonconfrontational questions. A useful approach is working from the assumption that the company comprises units, departments, and individuals who are committed to working with one another. Statements, positions, and events that convey divisiveness are puzzling within this context, prompting questions. A few nonconfrontational questions are not going to overcome divisiveness on their own, but they at least challenge the assumption that this is the only valid perspective within the organization.

See Table 7.2, which illustrates an action plan for implementing the objectives discussed in this section.

Community Objective: Unity

The remedy for the debilitating condition of personal alienation is feeling connected, feeling integrated and accepted into the large group, becoming part of a unified community.

The only way to create this unity is by literally joining with and caring about your fellow workers. And the best way to do that is to get out of yourself, have empathy, give of yourself, and support one another.

Building mutual support among employees is a fundamental step toward building a sense of community. Expressing support includes celebrating successes and sympathizing with frustrations. Mutual support conveys a welcoming attitude. Here are a few strategies to accomplish this:

Table 7.2.   Action Progress Form

Area of Work Life: Community
Problem: Poor Communication

The Objective	The Target	Actions	Time Line	Progress
1. Better communication	Reach out.	• Broaden informal contacts. • Plan communications. • Make ongoing contacts.	• 3 weeks • 2 weeks • 1 year	• • •
2. Better communication	Listen to messages.	• Evaluate organizational communications. • Select productive sources. • Establish dialogue.	• 3 months • 1 year • 1 year	• • •
3. Better communication	Ask questions.	• Attend to organizational communications. • Establish active dialogue.	• 3 months • 1 year	• •

Model Community Spirit. As with the objective of communication, you can contribute as an individual to a sense of positive community culture. By modeling positive actions, you make a small contribution to the organization's sense of community. Some of your colleagues within a hostile or fragmented work environment may be quite reasonable people on their own. Only within the disconnected environment of work do they revert to an uncommunicative defensive position. With a little encouragement, at least some may be happy to interact in a constructive, positive way. In addition to improving your odds of experiencing supportive interactions, you have the satisfaction of knowing that you have done your utmost to build the community. The following list suggests a few ways to encourage a supportive environment at work:

- *Express support.* You can express support for other employees. You can acknowledge their successes and sympathize with their frustrations. This strategy requires seeking information about what others are doing.

- *Ask for support.* In a cold or hostile work environment, people may feel it's inappropriate to be supportive. Once you open the door by asking for sympathy, company, help, or recognition, it may become a regular part of your relationship.

- *Welcome new employees.* The culture of a cold, unsupportive company can establish itself quickly on new members. Through casual expressions of hostility or indifference, a work environment can make new members feel unwelcome. It can encourage a cynical attitude from the very beginning. You can alleviate some of that hostility by maintaining an open, outgoing, positive attitude toward new members.

Even when you're working in a hostile environment, there are opportunities to develop the positive relationships that are the building blocks of community. You and the people with whom you work are looking for community in their work. The work on its own doesn't carry the day. Building a sense of community is a benefit to everyone.

Organize a Support Group. You can take community spirit an-other step up the scale by building a support group. To counter po-tential problems in divisiveness, the ideal support group crosses organizational boundaries. It might be associated with a workplace fitness program or some other regular function outside the normal work flow. The strategy is to develop an island of supportiveness in a bleak sea of unresponsiveness. By applying the qualities described previously, along with a group of like-minded colleagues, you can establish a positive trend in the organizational culture.

A support group can begin by attending solely to its members. If it successfully meets their needs over time, the group can reach out to others, inviting new members to join or help initiate similar groups.

Organize a Community Service Project. Many companies and organizations have an annual or quarterly public service workday, where everyone in the company goes and digs a ditch for the town's new irrigation program or paints a house for the halfway center group home. If your community isn't doing this already, there are many local and national organizations that can help you get started.

See Table 7.3, which illustrates an action plan for implement-ing the objectives discussed in this section.

General Guidelines

The following are useful points to consider in your efforts to build community. Your plan will be better informed by anticipating po-tential resistance to your initiatives, by building alliances with oth-ers in the organization, and by carefully considering the potential risks. Although the project does confront some serious challenges, the potential contribution to a sense of community at work justifies the effort and the risk.

Anticipate Resistance to Change

Building community presents special challenges regarding resis-tance to change in that the targets of your efforts are the attitudes and behaviors of the people who may be resistant. You can't really

Table 7.3. Action Progress Form

Area of Work Life: Community
Problem: Alienation

The Objective	The Target	Actions	Time Line	Progress
1. Unity	Model community spirit.	• Identify opportunities. • Model positive actions. • Welcome new employees.	• 3 weeks • 2 weeks • 1 year	• • •
2. Unity	Organize a support group.	• Assess potential allies. • Identify shared activities. • Recruit new members.	• 3 months • 1 year • 1 year	• • •
3. Unity	Organize a community service project.	• Identify potential causes. • Identify potential allies. • Initiate activity.	• 3 months • 1 year • 1 year	• • •

force them to be empathic, transparent, optimistic, happy, and supportive overnight. As the following list indicates, the lack of community is a serious gap that undermines in many ways the organization's capacity to pull itself out of its problems.

- A built-in problem for curing a dysfunctional community is that the ultimate means through which you are attempting to improve connectedness is the very same organization that isn't currently working. So external expertise and intervention may be necessary to overcome the challenge.

- Building mutual support in a hostile work environment is a serious challenge. People become deeply committed to their position in chronic conflicts. A history of coldness and hostility promotes cynicism on a group level that discourages anyone from attempting anything with positive implications. Introducing an upbeat agenda to a cynical group is an uphill battle.

- Communication strategies are difficult to implement. One serious impediment is the ease of communication. Most working people are flooded with messages, the huge majority of which are more important to the party sending the message than to anyone receiving it. People often prefer the risk of neglecting one important message to the burden of sorting through a hundred useless messages.

Build Alliances

When it comes to community, many people have the potential to help you. Building community is certainly not something you can do on your own. The project gains depth and momentum by including the perspectives and skills of others in the organization. The experience of working together on these initiatives is another step toward a sense of community.

As the following list indicates, there are potential allies for your efforts in the organization.

- New members of the organization enter without baggage from whatever conflicts led to the problems that the team is currently experiencing. They may arrive from settings that have a more constructive, positive approach to community. They are both allies and potential sources of expertise and experience.

- Support staff in human resources, planning, or training can be sources of expertise and moral support for efforts to improve communication. They would know who has expertise as a mediator or leader of off-site sessions.

- Senior management may be aware of chronic problems in the company's functioning. They may value any effort that gives effective operations a priority over perpetuating old grudges. This support can be powerful in accessing resources or in making efforts to make connectedness a high priority for the organization.

Assess Your Risks

Building community has relatively few pitfalls. Old friends may be miffed by your attempts to build new allegiances. Failed attempts to build allegiances can be discouraging and socially embarrassing. In most situations, these risks are fairly mild compared with continual isolation or conflict. The following list notes some of the potential hazards:

- Longtime members of a hostile organization may be locked into a position of hostility and cynicism that can be emotionally draining.

- Coworkers may be suspicious of your attempts at initiating a positive community spirit. Your attempts at promoting an upbeat attitude in new employees may prompt them to redouble their efforts of recruiting new employees to the dysfunctional culture.

- Your attempts to promote a mediation process may backfire, with the parties becoming even more deeply entrenched in their chronic conflicts.

Step Four: Tracking Progress

Use the Action Progress Form to track the development of your initiatives. A personal communication plan would benefit from a more detailed format, permitting you to identify targets, messages, responses, and time lines.

On a regular basis, revisit the items on community to determine whether you detect any signs of progress toward building a more supportive community at work.

An Illustrative Story

Kate, the vice president of Nursing Services, faced a serious crisis of community at Forrest Gate Hospital. A recent labor action by the nursing union at the hospital prompted the state government to pass back-to-work legislation and impose a salary settlement that was even worse than management's final offer to the union before they went on strike. Larger pay increases went to other unions and nonunion employees, who were not affected by the legislation. As a result, the nurses, who had made the case that they were the least adequately paid employee group at the hospital, received the worst settlement. The nurses were angry, resentful of other hospital sectors, and alienated.

Kate took on nursing administration because she believed nurses were marginalized in the power dynamics of the hospital. There were long-standing resentments between nurses and medical staff. There was a nearly impermeable wall between point-of-care nurses and management, with little communication flowing. Within the nursing structure, there were further divisions. There was little contact of surgical nurses with pediatric nurses with medical nurses with emergency nurses. They stayed primarily within their distinct groups. Kate recognized divisiveness as a big challenge before the recent events. Now it was at crisis proportions.

Following the Four Steps

Here's how Kate worked the four steps.

Step One: Defining the Problem: Divisiveness

There were many dimensions to the current crisis, but divisiveness was a core element.

Indications in the My Relationship with Work Test. Kate scored major mismatches on S8, S9, and S10, reflecting deep divisions between nursing and the rest of the hospital.

Step Two: Setting Objectives: Conflict Resolution

Kate's primary objective was to resolve the conflict of the nursing department with the rest of the organization. The legislation defined a time line of six months. If the parties had not reached a negotiated settlement by that time, the matter would go to binding arbitration. Kate was concerned that settling the matter through an external arbitrator would perpetuate the current divisiveness. It was greatly preferable for the two parties to resolve their problems together.

Step Three: Taking Action: Mediation

Through persuasive arguments, calling in favors, and all the leverage Kate could bring to her cause, she convinced the hospital board and the union executive to engage in a mediation initiative. The two parties identified an outside, professional mediator with extensive experience in labor issues and a successful track record of conflict resolution. The sessions were initiated well ahead of the six-month deadline and continued over six intense sessions. Throughout the negotiation process—which was hard-hitting and thorough—Kate returned to the theme that both groups would be stronger if they could create their own settlement than if they accepted one created by an arbitration panel or the legislature.

A month before the deadline, the two parties signed an agreement.

Step Four: Tracking Progress

Divisiveness remained a challenge at Forrest Gate Hospital, but the cohesiveness of the community was gradually improving. Kate believed the negotiation process to have made up much of the ground lost by the back-to-work legislation. The experience of resolving this fundamental issue provided a foundation for cross-boundary projects and other initiatives toward a more integrated, supportive work environment.

Chapter Eight

Solving Fairness Problems

Fairness and respect create a workplace where one can feel confident of the humanity and justice of the organization. It feels like a safe place to settle down, relax, and be contained by the virtue of the environment. Unfair treatment and disrespect push you to the periphery and beyond. Disrespect excludes you from what is going on. Unfairness promotes cynicism, undermining employees' relationships with work. It can be devastating to witness or be the victim of organizational injustice, to experience discrimination, to be on the short end of favoritism, or to have your talents overlooked in a decision crucial to your work life because someone dislikes something about you personally.

Unfairness can start from the top and permeate the entire corporate culture, or it can persist despite the values of the larger community, organizational policies, and legal regulations. Some instances of unfair treatment are no doubt due to individuals taking actions that put their self-interest above their responsibility to fair treatment. In other situations, individuals who believed that they scrupulously attended to the details of fair treatment find that their actions are perceived as reflecting bias and self-interest. When procedures are not transparent, it is difficult for individuals to determine whether they are being fairly treated.

Our concerns in the workplace include how we are treated personally as well as our perception of the fairness and respect that others receive. When fairness is a problem in an organization, that organization's capacity to operate as a coherent whole is compromised. And employees' quality of work life is diminished. The resulting cynicism aggravates the experience of burnout among employees.

Step One: Defining the Problem

Problems of *fairness* concern the general attitudes that people convey toward one another as well as the outcome of key workplace decisions.

Fairness Problem: Disrespect

A lack of respect at work is directly in conflict with a value of fair treatment. Interactions that demean or embarrass people damage their self-esteem. The negative impact can reverberate in the individual or the community for an extended time. For example, people may be abrupt and unfriendly in their interactions with you or insensitive to the impact of the jokes they tell. You may feel excluded from certain events (for example, the office poker game, informal get-togethers after work). In discussions, you are interrupted or ignored. Or people are just rude and make no effort to show respect to anyone except authority figures. Although some instances of disrespect are intentional, others reflect a lack of attention, poor etiquette, or ignorance by the person giving offense. A strong organizational culture strives to reduce the incidence and severity of both.

Indications in the My Relationship with Work Test. A lack of respect is noted by mismatches on F8, F9, and F10.

Fairness Problem: Discrimination

Discrimination involves biased actions toward people based on their personal characteristics (such as their race, ethnicity, gender, sexual orientation, disability, or age) rather than on their actual qualifications. These biases undermine organizational effectiveness by putting performance secondary to destructive personal agendas. They alienate the workplace community by denying the worth and integrity of some of its members. Discrimination also involves various forms of harassment, which make the job a very hostile and intimidating place to work. In such a situation, you or your colleague may be passed over for an obvious promotion, special perk, or opportunity in favor of someone with less qualification or experience. People tell jokes that cause others to feel uncomfortable or embarrassed or use demeaning insults or slurs in their conversations. Coworkers may get their way by bullying.

Indications in the My Relationship with Work Test. Discrimination is indicated by mismatches on F1, F2, and F3.

Fairness Problem: Favoritism

Favoritism introduces an uncritical inclination to favor certain individuals. It may be based on nepotism (favoring a family member), long-term friendship, or just plain personal whim. To the extent that favoritism exists or is tolerated, then some people will try to "play the game" to get that favored status (rather than getting recognized on the basis of merit). For example, you may have colleagues who engage in "sucking up" or "brownnosing" to get the boss's attention. Some may play fast and loose with the truth to get ahead (for example, they may pad their résumés, claim credit when it's not due them, or shift the blame to others for their own mistakes). The operational challenge to the organization is that people in positions of responsibility are allocating company positions or resources without regard to operational considerations. The emotional impact of favoritism is alienating to the larger proportion of employees who are not in favor.

Indications in the My Relationship with Work Test. Favoritism is indicated by mismatches on F4, F5, F6, and F7.

Step Two: Setting Objectives

When it comes to matters of fairness, we each are responsible for ensuring not only that we are treated fairly but that others are too.

Fairness Objective for Disrespect: Promoting Respect

The objective for the problem of disrespect goes beyond responding to incidents of thoughtlessness or rudeness to a culture that actively promotes civility and respect. It's not just preventing bad interactions, but it's encouraging a pleasant and fulfilling environment.

For an individual who is not necessarily in a position to set or enforce organizational policy, it's important to take unilateral action based on announced company standards and common courtesy.

Fairness Objective for Discrimination: Valuing Diversity

The objective of a company whose employees have experienced discrimination or who fear impending prejudice must be to go beyond addressing incidents of bigotry and promoting tolerance. An organizational environment is a community in which people learn, develop, and reflect on central values in their lives. A responsible corporate citizen takes the lead in promoting exemplary, forward-looking conduct.

And again, if any of us experience or observe discrimination because of race, ethnicity, gender, or sexual orientation, it's up to us to do something about it, because there are avenues of justice, both within and without the organization, to pursue. We can't take this lying down.

Fairness Objective for Favoritism: Ensuring Equity

Policies and procedures that promote equitable treatment discourage favoritism. When someone violates this aspect of fairness, it's usually pretty obvious, because everyone can see who's getting promoted or given the most desirable jobs, offices, special assignments.

But as with disrespect and discrimination, it is no longer socially acceptable or even legal to operate outside the prescribed guidelines, regulations, and laws of the land. If one of us blows the whistle, the results can be quick and effective. We can use the existing policies and legal requirements to our advantage. All we need is courage and initiative.

Step Three: Taking Action

Fairness and respect are issues calling for immediate action. Your experience of negative or hostile interactions is likely a sign of deep-seated problems in the organizational culture. These problems are the responsibility of management to address through procedures that are carefully monitored. It is also the responsibility of employees to respond in ways that call attention to this lack of fairness and convey that it is not acceptable.

Fairness Objective: Promoting Respect

There are various routes to promoting respect. Some respond to problem situations, others build positive alternatives for the long term.

Promote Civility. Etiquette is an excellent vehicle for promoting respect, developing attitudes, and teaching skills. Etiquette books are making a comeback. Young professionals, raised in a context of dining with the TV on and freedom from any dress codes (except those inflicted by their teenaged peers), realize that they don't know how to dine and dress in a serious business context. They may realize that they should not refer to a delegation of senior executives as "you guys," but they haven't a clue about more acceptable modes of address.

A discussion of the more-structured qualities of business etiquette could evolve into consideration of more fundamental qualities of being respectful of anyone whom they encounter in the course of their work life.

As noted previously, civility is a foundation for a sense of community at work. In an age when more than a few people are self-centered to a staggering degree, a concerted, well-designed effort may be necessary to ensure that employees become aware of and respectful of their coworkers' opinions, preferences, and points of view. Encouraging them to translate this newly found awareness into actions or words that convey respect, warmth, and positive regard takes the matter to a whole new level.

A training program along this line need not be heavy-handed. It can acknowledge that participants are aware that physical violence is not appropriate workplace behavior and move directly to actions and words that convey a positive, constructive quality to personal interactions at work.

Address Instances of Disrespect. An organizational culture of respect communicates a strong position that acts of rudeness, incivility, and disrespect are unacceptable in the workplace. There are a range of reactions that convey that message. Personal, informal reactions can be effective with unintentional, insensitive, or unconscious incidents that have little hostility and do not continue a pattern of continued offense. When there is a continued pattern of disrespectful incidents, more formal procedures are appropriate.

- *Talking about the incident.* When you experience an incident of disrespect, the most immediate response is to talk about it. Pointing out the problem may prompt an apology. It may be that the offending party is just plain ignorant, insensitive, and unaware that he or she is behaving in a way that could be interpreted as discriminatory or prejudiced, so the occasion could be a valuable learning experience. It's surprising how many people are unaware of the impact of certain words or attitudes or assumptions. If, however, there are any expressions of hostility, including persistence with the offensive actions, that may end the conversation. Arguments won't help, and returning offense may compromise your pursuit of official action.

- *Going to your supervisor.* Taking the matter to your supervisor brings the official standards of the organization into the discussion. Your supervisor can provide moral support for your discussions with the person causing offense or take the lead in the discussion for you. This can be valuable when the incident has been emotionally upsetting for you.

- *Going to your team.* If you work in a team-based work setting, it may be effective to take the issue to the team. This approach becomes more attractive when you're confident of active support from some of your team members. The team's response can be a more convincing statement that disrespect is unacceptable: it's not simply a supervisor stating the official management line but a view shared by coworkers in the organization.

- *Registering a complaint.* A persistent pattern of hostile responses to attempts to discuss the problem calls for stronger reactions. You may not be confident that your supervisor or work team will support you adequately in addressing the problem. You can use the organization's procedures for registering complaints. This approach requires careful preparation of your complaint, clarifying specific actions and words and noting the place and time of an incident as well as any witnesses. It helps to consult a friend to help you with preparing the complaint and to be supportive through the process.

Make Formal Complaints. If it gets to the point where the offending behaviors are becoming sufficiently hostile and threatening, then the matter has evolved to a problem of bullying and harassment. In the next section, we describe what you can do to get the organization to take more serious actions in this regard. And if the organization is unable or unwilling to address incidents of discrimination, the next step is taking the complaint to external organizations and government agencies or initiating legal action.

See Table 8.1, which illustrates an action plan for implementing the objectives discussed in this section.

Fairness Objective: Valuing Diversity

Valuing diversity is both an active promotion of workplace values and a mode for reacting to problem situations. Some situations are often complex and emotionally charged. Biases are often emotionally

Table 8.1.   Action Progress Form

Area of Work Life: Fairness
Problem: Disrespect

The Objective	The Target	Actions	Time Line	Progress
1. Promoting respect	Promote civility.	• Identify opportunities. • Identify training programs. • Participate in training programs.	• 3 weeks • 2 weeks • 1 year	• • •
2. Promoting respect	Address disrespect.	• Talk about incidents. • Involve supervisor. • Involve team. • Register complaints.	• 3 months • 1 year • 1 year • 1 year	• • • •
3. Promoting respect	Make formal complaints.	• Identify offenses. • Identify process for registering complaints. • Initiate process.	• 3 months • 1 year • 1 year	• • •

charged. People may be angry that you're offended. Handling situations effectively often calls for sound judgment on your part to find the appropriate response.

Get Training in Cultural Diversity. A mobile work world comprising people of highly diverse backgrounds who are working together is an occasion for all of us to learn and expand our horizons. If your organization or workplace community is having a problem dealing with diversity, however, it can become a very difficult and destructive situation that needs everyone's attention. The first step is often just plain education: we need to get to know one another better. All of us.

An initiative for cultural awareness and appreciation need not come from senior management. It is an initiative that could be promoted by employees anywhere in the organization who have a commitment to the issue. Valuing diverse cultures is something that in a way trumps the chain of command.

There are many attractive entry points to cultural awareness, with food and music near the top of the list for accessible topics. Cultural perspectives on business etiquette may be an attractive entry point for some companies.

Use Internal Procedures. Many organizations already have specific procedures for registering complaints of bullying, mobbing, abuse, or other forms of discrimination or harassment. Usually, the most readily available point for registering a problem is with one's immediate supervisor. There may even be a designated position of equity officer or ombudsman to provide an option for action outside the normal reporting structure.

Registering official complaints is necessary for those of us who are experiencing or observing unfairness. It is possible that an abusive person will interpret a response of quiet resignation as indicating that abuse and bullying is tolerated in the work setting. A quick response from a sanctioned office for addressing these problems may be a timely and powerful educational experience.

Use External Procedures. If organizational procedures are inadequate, there are mechanisms outside the organization through unions, professional groups, human rights organizations, and local, regional, state, and federal civil rights offices that specialize in enforcing the law. Individuals on many levels have recourse to legal action in response to discrimination. There are organizations and community groups that can advise on such procedures or assist in legal costs.

Instituting legal procedures can be difficult and disruptive in your life. These procedures rarely go smoothly and always proceed slowly. But it may be a necessary step in developing the organization's commitment to promoting respectful conduct. In other words, if your group can't deal with this themselves, they're going to have to answer to a more public and official investigation and possible legal suit.

A problematic legal case can point out the advantages of effective internal procedures in a compelling fashion. Few CEOs or directors of Human Resources would relish the task of justifying an organization's tolerance of abusive interactions among employees.

See Table 8.2, which illustrates an action plan for implementing the objectives discussed in this section.

Fairness Objective: Ensuring Equity

Ensuring fair treatment requires good procedures and a willingness to use them when you or others are denied equitable treatment on important decisions.

Insist on Clear Procedures. Your organization's hiring and promotion procedures may be structured in ways that make them vulnerable to favoritism. Without a firm policy on announcing the availability of a new position, it may only be evident to a select few. Without clearly articulated job requirements, a manager could decide to emphasize a set of skills and perspectives in a subset of the candidates. The unstructured job interview continues to be used in many settings despite considerable evidence of its susceptibility to

Table 8.2. Action Progress Form

Area of Work Life: Fairness
Problem: Discrimination

The Objective	The Target	Actions	Time Line	Progress
1. Valuing diversity	Get training in cultural diversity.	• Identify programs. • Encourage participation. • Discuss relevance with coworkers.	• 3 weeks • 2 weeks • 1 year	• • •
2. Valuing diversity	Use internal procedures.	• Assess incidents. • Assess internal procedures. • Register complaints.	• 3 months • 1 year • 1 year	• • •
3. Valuing diversity	Use external procedures.	• Assess incidents. • Assess internal procedures. • Register complaints.	• 3 months • 1 year • 1 year	• • •

bias and its poor track record in identifying candidates who are ultimately successful in a position. The primary outcome of an unstructured interview is the interviewers' assessment of how comfortable they felt with each candidate. People tend to feel comfortable with people who are a lot like them. That does little to promote a diversity agenda for the organization.

Any decision about bonuses or perks that moves from a manager's individual decision to a group consideration becomes more equitable and rigorous.

A component of a fair decision-making process is an appeal process. Appeal procedures introduce a means of ensuring that the procedures for guaranteeing equitable consideration actually occurred. It also provides an opportunity for a second consideration of the decision. Even if the appeal is not successful, it ensures that the process was conducted in an appropriate manner.

Encourage Workshops on Recruitment and Promotion Procedures. Hiring procedures are rule-bound social interactions, the fine points of which escape many individuals, who nonetheless want an active participation in employment decisions.

The training can not only acquaint participants with the specific policies and legal considerations on hiring, it can also emphasize the participants' responsibilities to an equitable process in which the requirements for the position are the definitive issues in the hiring decision. The training can emphasize as well the benefits and challenges of an increasingly diverse workforce.

Promote Transparency. Talk about the allocation of perks, benefits, and promotions with colleagues. These things work out more fairly when everyone is aware of who is allocating what. In disseminating this information, you may be relinquishing your inside track to certain rewards for yourself. In the long run, a more open, equitable allocation of perks and benefits is likely to be in everyone's best interest, including your own.

See Table 8.3, which illustrates an action plan for implementing the objectives discussed in this section.

Table 8.3.   Action Progress Form

Area of Work Life: Fairness
Problem: Favoritism

The Objective	The Target	Actions	Time Line	Progress
1. Ensuring equity	Have clear procedures.	• Examine internal procedures. • Research cases of improved procedures. • Encourage discussion on change.	• 3 weeks • 2 weeks • 1 year	• • •
2. Ensuring equity	Encourage workshops.	• Assess potential trainers. • Encourage presentations. • Encourage participation. • Discuss application.	• 3 months • 1 year • 1 year • 1 year	• • • •
3. Ensuring equity	Promote transparency.	• Identify procedures and practices. • Encourage general discussion.	• 3 months • 1 year	• •

General Guidelines

The following are general guidelines for addressing issues of fairness. These are loaded issues for individuals personally and for organizations collectively. Enhancing the organization's procedure and culture with regard to respect and diversity will be significant challenges requiring careful preparation.

Anticipate Resistance to Change

Discrimination and many forms of disrespect at work are explicitly contrary to organizational policies and often illegal as well. Yet they continue to be real, powerful, and persistent problems in workplaces in the twenty-first century. The following list indicates some of the reasons for resistance to change:

- Prejudices are resistant to change. They are irrational and often emotionally charged. People who are deeply committed to their prejudices are capable of dismissing cogent argument, training, and factual information.

- Official complaints can advance slowly toward an inconclusive conclusion. An organization may have to experience a series of complaints that go through a tedious process of resolution before realizing that it has a systemic problem in need of an extensive, active response.

- Individuals may be wary of making complaints. They may feel that registering a complaint singles them out for suspicion and contempt.

- Disrespect and unfairness are shared problems. They reflect something wrong with an organization's culture. The well-being of employees is low on the list of priorities of some organizations. Your employer may not care about you or others like you. It may be confident that new talent is readily available. It may be confident that It can maintain a high level of performance without the dedication of individual employees. Its successes up to now may have given it too much confidence: the confidence has turned into arrogance.

Build Alliances

Although this certainly sounds grim, it does not mean that you're alone. Unfairness and disrespect are shared problems. If you're experiencing them, others are too. A sense of valuing others as individuals is pervasive. So others share your problem, and others will benefit from an improvement.

As the following list indicates, there are others in the organization and beyond for whom unfairness and disrespect are serious problems whose resolution is worthy of effort and resources.

- CEOs want to lead workplaces that are characterized by respect and fairness. In our consulting work, whenever we have pointed out to CEOs that many of their employees perceive important management decisions to indicate favoritism, they have taken quick action to counter that perception. Through effective communication and clear procedures, they were successful in doing so.
- Managers responsible for human resource issues in the organization will be allies in efforts to address these problems. They have resources and contacts to access expertise for training or consulting.
- Other employees in your organization will likely share your experiences of unfavoritism, disrespect, or discrimination. It will be possible to find active allies for a number of the initiatives discussed previously.

Assess Your Risks

Addressing issues of respect and fairness is a sensitive business. Suggestions that management is acting unfairly can be hard to make. Few organizations want to hear that they condone treating employees in a dismissive fashion. Accusations of unfairness and disrespect would reflect poorly on management from the perspective of their board of directors or its peer organizations.

Discrimination based on a wide range of employees' personal characteristics—race, gender, religion, and so forth—is illegal, providing the basis of formal proceedings against the company. In some circumstances, legal proceedings may serve to address the problem. But legal proceedings can also be disruptive to everyone involved. They do not always lead to clear or positive conclusions. In fact, we've all heard of times when whistle-blowers are the first to be fired.

You risk offending anyone who you suggest is acting unfairly or with disrespect. Although the organization's culture does not fully realize a people-centered culture, individuals usually think of themselves as fair-minded, civil individuals.

When pursuing a formal complaint against the organization—through the courts, union grievance committees, or a human rights tribunal—you can find yourself in an ongoing legal process. This can consume vast amounts of personal time, identify you as troublesome, and cost money.

The risks of addressing these problems are real. Placed against an ongoing experience of unfairness and disrespect, however, they may seem relatively modest.

Step Four: Tracking Progress

Your focus may be entirely on reducing the frequency or intensity of negative events at work. These are important events to track, to note if your efforts have led to fewer signs of disrespect or unfair treatment. It is important as well to track the incidence of positive alternatives. You need to replace the negative events with a positive alternative. After you've challenged people on disrespectful actions, they may think it best to avoid you. That's not really the point.

In some situations, your progress may be obvious. But sometimes you have to look closely to assess progress. And sometimes you need an accurate record to remember how different things used to be.

Are things improving? Along the way, it is useful to record your implementation of the action plan and reactions of clients, coworkers, managers, and the company in general to your initiatives.

In the final column of the Action Progress Form, note the dates on which you implemented each of the steps.

An Illustrative Story

Tom's career plans have been derailed. A week after he had applied for a promotion as evening-shift supervisor for the automobile assembly plant, he was asked to meet with the plant director, Fred. Tom was confident that his application was going to be well received. When the director's assistant arranged this meeting, Tom was expecting a first step in the selection process. Instead it was the last.

Fred politely, firmly, and coldly informed Tom that his application was not going to be pursued. Tom wasn't going to be interviewed. The view of the hiring committee was that despite his obvious talents and experience he had not yet developed the maturity expected of a supervisor.

Tom sat speechless for a full minute. He then said, "So is this meeting over?"

"Yes, Tom," answered Fred, "unless, of course, you have any questions."

"I have one question."

"Yes."

"My lack of 'maturity.' Is that because my parents are East Indian or because I'm gay?"

"Tom," Fred stated emphatically, "that has nothing to do with this decision."

Tom wasn't convinced.

Following the Four Steps

Here's how Tom worked the four steps.

Step One: Defining the Problem: Favoritism

Tom wasn't sure why he was refused a promotion into management. It could be because of his cultural background or sexual orientation. Or it could be because of his high-profile work with the union. As the only internal candidate and with considerable experience from this factory and his previous work in similar facilities, he believed that the stated rationale for rejecting his application—insufficient management maturity—was bogus.

Indications in the My Relationship with Work Test. Tom scored mismatches on many items, with F2, F3, and F4 as major mismatches.

Step Two: Setting Objectives: Ensuring Equity

In pursuing an equity complaint against management, Tom preferred going to an equity officer over going to the union. He wasn't sure how enthusiastically a union would support his bid to become part of management. And he figured this wasn't a good time to emphasize his connection with the union.

Step Three: Taking Action: Negotiating Better Assignments

Tom decided to get help and went to Wilbur, the company equity officer. Wilbur interviewed Tom in detail about his application, his background, and his conversation with Fred. Wilbur determined that there was sufficient question to warrant a review of the process. He confirmed that Tom was willing to see the process through.

Tom decided to proceed. He was reluctant to put this unfair decision behind him because of the affront to his personal sense of fairness. He also saw the process as a means of reemphasizing the company's commitment to fairness as an institutional value. He accepted the potential repercussions of an unsuccessful challenge. If it was established that he could be excluded from career advancement in this way, he would pursue his career elsewhere, regardless of the inconvenience and risk involved in leaving his job at the factory.

The equity process prompted a review of the promotion process. An evaluation of Tom's application against the formal criteria for the position determined that the decision to eliminate him from the competition was unfounded. It did not reference accurately the criteria that were defined in the position posting. "Maturity" was not referenced in the posting, and it was not defined in the company's policies. Fred maintained that other issues of attitude and professional maturity were relevant to decisions on advancement to management. The equity review judged that these criteria were too vague and subjective to justify the decision to exclude Tom from the process. Not only that, Tom had an excellent record for initiative and productivity in his work for the company to date.

Step Four: Tracking Progress

The process resulted in Tom receiving the promotion. His feeling of success was tempered somewhat by the fact that the position reported directly to Fred. And there was no clear answer to Tom's question of why he was excluded. It could have been cultural background, sexual orientation, or union activity.

The process gave Tom a new respect for the company's equity procedures. His scores on F2, F3, and F4 improved considerably over the following months. And he maintained a cordial, if somewhat cool, working relationship with Fred.

Chapter Nine

Solving Values Problems

These days, many organizations spend a lot of time and energy devising elaborate and finely crafted mission statements that articulate their values and goals for the public. And even if they don't, organizations intrinsically operate on and express a certain culture and set of policies that pursue a mission based on a set of values.

Values are evident in the organization's choices. For example, some corporations value long-term growth over quarterly profits. Others choose the opposite. In the entertainment industry, some corporations value their impact on global culture; others value bottom-line profit regardless of cultural impact.

Closely related to corporate values are ethical standards that guide the conduct of employees and define the propriety of the company's activities. Organizations vary in the thoroughness with which they articulate codes of conduct. In some organizations, ethical concerns are an ongoing topic of discussion; others are content to point at an industry manual with which their managers have only a passing acquaintance. They also vary in the sincerity of their stated intentions to comply with their standards and in the rigor with which they monitor compliance.

Individuals are capable of just as wide a variation in their values and their concern for ethical conduct. There is no single solution for everyone. Some would be appalled working for a company with shoddy ethical standards whereas others would find a rigorous monitoring of ethical conduct to be intrusive and deadening. In either direction, a serious mismatch on ethical standards can be an ongoing irritant, undermining relationships with work, leading ultimately to burnout.

Similarly, a mismatch on values means that the company is involved in pursuits that you consider to be damaging, offensive, or simply trivial. It is not how you want to spend you life. Your efforts at work are either a waste of time or a betrayal of deeply held convictions. This is exhausting in that there is no meaningful confirmation from your work; it's just effort down the drain. If you can't become genuinely involved in activities that run contrary to your values, you can become pretty darn cynical. It's hard to gain a sense of effectiveness or accomplishment from work that you believe is trivial, wasteful, or harmful. A values mismatch has all the ingredients of a crisis in burnout: exhaustion, cynicism, and ineffectiveness.

Step One: Defining the Problem

The three primary forms of *values* mismatches are concerns about dishonesty, destructive activities, and meaninglessness. You may experience any or all of these mismatches at a given time.

Values Problem: Dishonesty

Corporate dishonesty has received considerable media attention in recent years. Acts of self-serving dishonesty and greed on the part of senior executives in major corporations ruined businesses and the financial well-being of their employees and their stockholders. The failure of regulatory agencies and audits by major accounting firms to monitor and curtail this abuse undermined public confidence in the corporate world. In the course of your job, you may be directed to do things that are illegal and dishonest. When this happens, you're confronted with a serious dilemma between your job security and your integrity.

Indications in the My Relationship with Work Test. Dishonesty is noted by mismatches on V1, V2, V3, V4, and V5.

Values Problem: Destructiveness

The activities of businesses, small and large, have a potential destructive impact on their employees and on the larger community. Through development projects, corporations in property development, energy, and primary resource development have wreaked havoc on the environment. When they are constrained in their exploitation at home, some of this activity is exported offshore. They leave the world worse than they found it.

This kind of destruction is not confined to companies that are blatant and abusive in their pollution of the air or water but really applies to all organizations and businesses that are not *sustainable*— that is, that don't leave the world exactly as they find it in terms of environmental quality or natural resources. Even a book publisher, for example, uses up more paper and trees than it recycles or is replanted. So eventually, we'll run out of paper. And it's well-known that such sustainability is extremely difficult to accomplish and not ordinarily the top priority of every operation, particularly if it's competing in a market where pricing is a major factor. Sustainability means higher costs and smaller margins.

Although contrary to your personal values, activities that have a destructive impact—directly or indirectly—may be part of your job. You are using your talents, time, and experience to make the world a worse place.

Indications in the My Relationship with Work Test. Destructiveness is indicated by mismatches on V6, V7, and V8.

Values Problem: Meaninglessness

Some jobs are platforms to save lives, educate eager students, or improve the quality of life in your community. Other jobs are not. They just pay the bills. And even though they may not pay the bills all that generously, it's hard to identify any reason other than a paycheck for continuing to go to work. The job may not be doing anything obviously destructive or hurtful. It just cranks out products—perhaps low-cost decorative items of no great quality. Just bits of fluff.

So you find yourself devoting a large percentage of your life to an activity that appears to be contributing nothing of importance to you or anyone else. This is a value conflict.

Indications in the My Relationship with Work Test. Unsatisfying work is indicated by mismatches on V9 and V10.

Step Two: Setting Objectives

Your objectives for value crises are to seek greater congruence between your values and those of your workplace. There are various routes toward these resolutions. Some address an immediate crisis in your work; others are struggles that continue throughout your working life. They all have an impact on the depth and quality of your relationship with work.

Values Objective for Dishonesty: Maintaining Integrity

There are situations in which you are pulled in conflicting directions, feeling uncertain of the right thing to do. Other situations are clear trade-offs between integrity and practical concerns. When confronting these choices, a core challenge is maintaining integrity.

Values Objective for Destructiveness: Promoting Constructive Values

A viable objective when contending with an employer with a destructive agenda is to promote a contrary, constructive set of values.

Values Objective for Meaninglessness: Adding Meaning

When your work in itself doesn't further what you value, you can search for ways of adding meaning. This may occur in the context of your job or in additional activities not associated with the workplace or with colleagues.

Step Three: Taking Action

Pursuing your values at work comes down to taking action. Your values don't become fully yours until you act on them. The most definitive situation in which to define your values through action occurs when you're confronting a value conflict.

Values Objective: Maintaining Integrity

You can find yourself confronted with ethical dilemmas out of the blue. For example, after working at a company for a few years, your boss directs you to charge a client's account with expenses that were not incurred. Or you could be well aware that colleagues and managers were up to their necks in questionable dealings. You know it's an issue that you're going to confront sooner or later, but you don't know when. In either situation, giving the matters some forethought prepares you to manage the situation.

A Focus on Ethical Dilemmas.   You can take action before a crisis or conflict occurs. You could develop a forum on business ethics at work. It could be an informal conversation group among interested colleagues. It could be a program conducted by the training division. A case-oriented course on handling ethical dilemmas familiarizes you with the challenge of weighing competing options. It also makes a statement about the company's position on ethical issues, including its commitment to maintaining high standards of conduct.

For example, a group of employees in the accounting department of a company that sold air-conditioning systems became increasingly concerned about a pattern of reporting among the sales reps. The same expense would appear on several accounts. Items appeared on invoices that were outside the range of services on the contract. Some of the problem entries could have resulted from poor attention to detail, but others looked like deliberate padding. The pattern began with one or two people in sales. After a while, it was a problem with the reports of most sales reps.

The accounting group preferred to take a positive approach to this growing problem. The director of the finance unit met with the director of sales to indicate the scope and seriousness of the problem. Rather than take punitive action, the accounting group proposed bringing in a trainer to run a series on ethical decision making. The director of sales agreed to require the participation of the sales reps in the series.

Confrontation. When directed to act unethically, you could respond in various ways. One option is to take a stand on ethical grounds, articulate your position, and challenge the other party to defend the directive to act unethically. For example, if you're an attorney and one of the upper-level partners in the firm bills for more hours at higher rates than are actually warranted, you can state your judgment of the unethical nature of this action and ask for an explanation. If nothing else, this step provides a reality check: you might have misread the situation.

This action, although challenging your direct superior, is not as audacious as it might appear at first. People—even people in senior positions—are somewhat tentative about engaging in unethical, illegal behavior. It's obvious to everyone that something underhanded is happening, and there is a keen interest in keeping underhanded activities under wraps. So there is a good possibility that your boss will back down.

If not, and if the request becomes even more insistent, you've gained valuable information. Your future in this firm depends on engaging in unethical, illegal activities. It's generally a good thing to know before you invest much more of your time and abilities in this organization. This is a point at which to consider your priorities: you balance your job security against your commitment to ethical standards. When faced with such choices, people make their choice based on their values.

Whistle-Blowing. Whistle-blowing is taking a very strong position, and it requires great courage. We've all heard of such individuals getting the ax. You're going outside the organization to authorities with the capacity to make the company accountable for its actions. The process requires diligence, careful preparation, and persistence.

- Preliminary research is needed to identify the proper authorities to contact and the procedures for doing so.
- Your research can include other whistle-blowing events in your industry, noting the process and the outcome.
- It's important to review the evidence. Investigations of corporate wrongdoing demand rigorous standards of evidence.
- Involvement in legal procedures goes more smoothly with expert advice.

As noted at the beginning of this section, your values don't become fully yours until you act on them. An action as definitive as whistle-blowing will let you and others know where you stand on at least a few important values.

See Table 9.1, which illustrates an action plan for implementing the objectives discussed in this section.

Values Objective: Promoting Constructive Values

This approach may comprise parallel activities that compensate for the company's continuing destructive behavior as well as initiatives to reduce the company's pursuit of destructive actions. Although you may not be able to attain a state of "no harm done," you may be able to attain "less harm done."

Change the Company's Values. You may work to change the values of your company. This seems like an ambitious concept. But there may be something to gain from a struggle in support of central values in your life. There likely is a wide range of actions you can take to state a position against your company's contribution to environmental degradation. You need not start with chaining yourself to

Table 9.1. Action Progress Form

Area of Work Life: Values
Problem: Dishonesty

The Objective	The Target	Actions	Time Line	Progress
1. Maintaining integrity	A focus on ethical dilemmas	• Identify training resources. • Encourage discussions among coworkers. • Maintain general awareness.	• 6 months • 6 months • 1 year	• • •
2. Maintaining integrity	Confrontation	• Recognize incidents. • Clarify your ethical position or professional code of ethics. • Confront ethical challenges.	• 3 months • 1 year • 1 year	• • •
3. Maintaining integrity	Whistle-blowing	• Identify offenses. • Identify process for registering complaints. • Initiate process.	• 3 months • 1 year • 1 year	• • •

the bulldozers. You can take actions that engage a dialogue without immediately jeopardizing your employment status.

The important point is for the issue to be discussed. Through informal conversations, official meetings, and educational programs, the topic can be emphasized as a central consideration for the company. In the example of environmental impact, extensive discussions may reveal that senior management is seriously concerned with environmental impact, is making serious investments in mitigating the damage, and is equally frustrated with the slowness of the time line. This would be a different context for your values conflict than one in which senior management was oblivious or hostile to environmental considerations. The primary point is that engaging a dialogue that confronts value conflicts provides an opening for resolution.

Make Up for the Damage. If one cannot stop the damaging impact of a company's activities, one can work to mitigate its impact. For example, a mining company can refill and restore a landscape after closing a strip-mining operation. The original habitat has definitely been destroyed, but reshaped and replanted landscape is a clear improvement over a slag heap. These balancing schemes raise questions, as resource development companies are accused of being stingy. Cleanup or restitution efforts are condemned as trivial gestures in contrast to the enormity of their damage. And critics contend that these actions are attempts to manage public opinion, not altruistic acts. The issue for your participation in activities that compensate for previous damage by the company is whether your direct involvement reduces the mismatch between your personal values and those of the company.

Pursue Parallel, Constructive Activities. A variation on the previous approach is to pursue constructive activities to balance the more damaging parts of the operation. The difference is that these activities do not necessarily undo the damage. But they do something positive in another domain. For example, an urban property development firm can establish a playground for children. This activity does not address problems arising from its development activities. It makes a positive contribution to a neighborhood.

Contemporary corporations are diverse. Their record of activity is often so complex and dispersed that it is difficult to compute a comprehensive list of the corporation's impact across the country or around the world. A resolution is more readily available when there is latitude in selecting the activities to support through your contribution. While working on a long-term objective of changing the corporate agenda in a positive direction, you can engage in activities that help offset any negative impact from other areas of the company's operations.

See Table 9.2, which illustrates an action plan for implementing the objectives discussed in this section.

Values Objective: Adding Meaning

There are many ways to add meaning to your work life.

Adding Exceptional Quality.   You can bring meaning to work that at first appears to have little to offer. People derive meaning from how they work, not only what they do. You can produce products or service of exceptional quality. Meaning is evident in the process rather than the content.

- For example, the process of serving doughnuts cheerfully and attentively can be a valuable contribution to the customer, outweighing the nutritional shortcomings of the product being served.
- Craftspeople and artists raise mundane objects—bowls, candlesticks, and the like—to another level of significance through excellent work and design.
- A job of modest dimensions can be a valuable learning experience, preparing an employee for positions of greater responsibility with the same company or elsewhere. Meaning can be

Table 9.2.   Action Progress Form

Area of Work Life: Values
Problem: Destructiveness

The Objective	The Target	Actions	Time Line	Progress
1. Promoting constructive values	Change company values.	• Identify values in practice. • Initiate discussions. • Heighten concern with corporate image.	• 3 weeks • 2 weeks • 1 year	• • •
2. Promoting constructive values	Compensate for damage.	• Talk about corporate impact. • Promote concept of responsibility. • Develop with coworkers potential repair strategies.	• 3 months • 1 year • 1 year	• • •
3. Promoting constructive values	Pursue parallel activities.	• Recognize negative impact. • Identify potential constructive initiatives. • Promote constructive action.	• 3 months • 1 year • 1 year	• • •

found in the process of learning. The focus can be on performing well rather than on the outcome of the performance.

Doing Charitable Work. You can add meaningfulness through extra activities. This is a worthy strategy even if you are confident in the value of your work. You can take the initiative by involving your workplace in a charitable cause. You can participate as an individual or with a few friends from work, or you can lobby for the charity to receive official support from the company on a regular basis. Even if the charity is unrelated to the business of the company, it could benefit from the energy of capable people. Your direct participation is usually necessary for this strategy to have a personal impact on value matches. Just knowing that the corporation that employs you made a contribution to the college building fund or to a summer camp for chronically ill children may not be enough, despite the impressive scale of the contribution.

Changing Your Job. If none of these strategies are appropriate to your situation, it may be time to consider a new job. If you have deeply held values and principles that are impossible to fulfill in your present situation, then determine where you could pursue those values more effectively. It may be difficult to move directly to a position in that setting. Your present position or an intermediate position could serve as a means for positioning yourself for the move to your preferred workplace. As noted previously, in the section Adding Exceptional Quality, the process of learning in a job is a basis for meaningfulness.

Jobs are not forever. We often change jobs many times over the course of a career. We get fired, get laid off, get promoted, get better offers, get fed up and quit. It happens all the time. Even if you're convinced that you must stay with your current job, chances are you won't. So it makes sense to find and position yourself for jobs that offer a better match with your core values.

See Table 9.3, which illustrates an action plan for implementing the objectives discussed in this section.

Table 9.3.   Action Progress Form

Area of Work Life: Values
Problem: Meaninglessness

The Objective	The Target	Actions	Time Line	Progress
1. Adding meaning	Adding exceptional quality.	• Review frequent tasks. • Identify essential qualities. • Work with attention to quality.	• 3 weeks • 2 weeks • 1 year	• • •
2. Adding meaning	Doing charitable work.	• Identify potential charities. • Discuss with coworkers. • Organize events.	• 3 months • 1 year • 1 year	• • •
3. Adding meaning	Changing your job.	• Identify opportunities. • Explore potential for value congruence. • Pursue specific positions.	• 3 months • 1 year • 1 year	• • •

General Guidelines

Consider the following guidelines for solving values problems.

Anticipate Resistance to Change

Organizational values don't change quickly or easily. Values are at the core of a company's identity and culture. They are reinforced by its history, its policies, its financial plan, and its strategies. For example, for a mining company to operate in accordance with higher standards of environmental stewardship, it must make significant capital investments, develop new procedures, and create a new financial plan. The company has to address the challenge of competing with other companies that have not made similar investments. Changes of heart on this scale happen, but not quickly. As the following list indicates, resistance can occur at many levels of the organization.

- Initiatives to raise the ethical standards of an organization will encounter resistance from individuals or groups who benefit from the status quo. Businesses become dependent on unethical practices, losing their capacity to operate profitably on a legitimate basis.
- Constructive activities require investment. Plans that go outside the company's business plan require new skills and installations. The process of including these within the overall business plan can be painfully slow.
- Introducing quality into your products and services can meet direct resistance from supervisors. Many operations are judged solely on speed rather than on quality.

Build Alliances

Your first allies in dealing with value conflicts are people who share your values. Second are people who believe in employees' freedom to follow their principles, even though they may not share your personal values. A third group of potential allies are those who agree that the organization fails to be true to its own values.

Often value conflicts arise because people who were initially attracted to an organization because of its stated values—challenging education, excellent patient care, customer-centered banking—conclude that these statements are a mere sham for expediency or for short-term profit orientations. Their value conflict is not so much between personal and organizational values but between stated ideas and realized ideals. If this is the basis of your disenchantment with the organization, you likely have many potential allies. If no one else agrees with your assessment of organizational insincerity, it would be good to double-check. Such departures are rarely so subtle that only one person can see them.

Assess Your Risks

Challenging a company's commitment to ethical principles or to its core values can prompt a serious reaction.

- Corporations like to present themselves as making a constructive contribution to the larger community. A reputation as a sincere and positive force in the community is a real asset in a corporation's business plan, especially in a time of widespread distrust of corporations. When challenging a company's commitment, you may have to contend with people whose full-time job is defending the company's position and making you look irresponsible, uninformed, and wrong.

- Whistle-blowers are subject to severe criticism, threats, and legal action. The film *Silkwood* powerfully depicts the difficulties and strains of this role.

- A company with a single focus on maximizing production and increasing profits will have little patience with attempts to increase quality. Spending additional time attending to customers may deepen your level of service in a meaningful way but may prompt serious criticism from your boss.

Step Four: Tracking Progress

Are things improving? Along the way, it is useful to record your implementation of the action plan and the reactions of clients, coworkers, managers, and the company in general to your initiatives.

In the final column of the Action Progress Form, note the dates on which you implemented each of the steps.

An Illustrative Story

Hector, a loans officer in a suburban branch of a major bank, is a great fan of banks. And the bigger the bank, the better. Unlike many of his peers, Hector was not nervous about the astounding concentration of capital wealth. He admired the power it represented. But even Hector had his limits.

Hector was committed to the bank's potential to be a positive service in the life of his clients. He believed that small business loans and mortgages were the means through which people developed opportunities and increased the quality of their lives. He played a role in helping them gain access to the necessary resources to fulfill their aspirations while making sure that they didn't get in over their heads in debt. Yes, debt tied people down, but Hector's conclusion was that people really didn't mind being tied down all that much. While pursuing what he saw as the constructive side of retail banking, Hector was adept at sidestepping the parts of the job that had less obvious benefit to customers.

But the new branch manager, Ron, had upset the balance in Hector's work life. His ideas were bigger, his ambitions unlimited, and his capacity to persevere unending. And his pet idea for personal banking amounted to promoting a range of services that his customers really didn't need. Hector was supposed to encourage individuals to open additional accounts and have separate credit cards for each family member and other features that would add a minimum of convenience at an increased monthly rate. Other services would organize credit card purchases into designated categories. This tidied up the account report, but the level of activity for most customers was so modest that the service did not justify its cost. But it turned a nice profit for the bank. Hector thought these services were at best a waste of time and likely actually harmful to his customers.

Ron didn't just suggest that Hector actively promote these services. He met with the account managers every day for updates on their efforts. Every day! It was getting hard to make it through these meetings without a confrontation. The other three loans officers at the branch were enthusiastically signing people up for these services. They had graphs that showed their blue, green, and yellow line creeping upward month by month, while Hector's orange line trailed far behind, even dropping lower some months. A confrontation was clearly brewing and Hector was not confident that it would go well for him.

Following the Four Steps

Here's how Hector worked the four steps.

Step One: Defining the Problem: Destructiveness

Hector was in a value conflict. He didn't mind the bank making a profit. He really liked the idea of contributing to the bank making a profit. But he wanted the bank to do something truly useful along the way. Hector had structured his work life on values that he shared with the bank: helping small businesses develop and helping individuals build homes. The current crisis pressured Hector to promote services that he saw as benefiting only the bank to the detriment of the customer.

Indications in the My Relationship with Work Test. Hector scored matches on many items. He shared many of the bank's values. But he scored major mismatches on V9 and V10, reflecting his conflict over marketing the new services, which he saw as harmful.

Step Two: Setting Objectives:
Promoting Constructive Values

Hector chose to promote constructive values. He accepted that the profit motive was an essential element of banking. He just wanted to ensure that the bank earned those profits by doing something useful.

Step Three: Taking Action: Changing the Company's Values

Hector decided to tackle the problem directly by going to Ron. They had a lively discussion. Hector described his reservations about promoting unnecessary services; Ron laid out his objectives for enhancing the performance of the branch. It was soon evident that each of them was committed to his position. But they both could appreciate the other's point of view. Ron knew that solid customer relationships were critical for the branch's success. Hector recognized that unless the branch made a positive financial contribution, its future would be in jeopardy.

They eventually reached a compromise. Hector agreed that he would increase his productivity in the areas where he was committed—small business loans and personal loans. Ron agreed to stop pressuring Hector to sell the new services. The resolution got Hector out of a direct involvement with the new services, but he was aware that other loans officers in the branch were promoting them. Ron agreed to forgo the profits that Hector might have produced with the new services but accepted Hector's commitment to increase performance on loans. The loans would not produce as great a profit as the new services. Ron would have to justify the branch's performance to his boss as both improved bottom-line profit and a more solid, enduring customer base.

Step Four: Tracking Progress

The process resulted in a truce between Ron and Hector. They maintained a positive working relationship over the next two years, until Ron moved on to a position with the regional office.

His scores on V9 and V10 moved to a match a year later.

Chapter Ten

Changing Your Relationship

So now you have developed an action plan, using one of the six strategies, which will help you improve your relationship with work and reduce burnout. Congratulations, and keep up the good work over the coming months! Remember that a relationship is ongoing and evolving, so you want to continue shaping it and moving it in the direction that you want it to go.

As we have been saying all along, your plan will take time, effort, and persistence before you begin to see the payoff. Although it is important to stick with your plan and not give up too soon, it is also important to be flexible and open to modifying it on the basis of relevant feedback and experience. What is critical is to keep your selected objective in mind and to use a variety of ways, if necessary, to achieve your long-term goal.

Keeping Your Eye on the Prize

Banish burnout! That is the reason why you are trying to change your relationship with work. It is a big challenge; it unfolds over a long time and requires considerable effort. What we have worked to provide you in this book are guidelines to ensure that your time and effort were well directed. If you've been struggling with burnout, you didn't have a lot of time and effort to lose!

Sticking with It

A commitment to an action plan is a commitment to the relationship between It and you: you really want to make the relationship work. There is a lot about your job that is important to you, and you don't want to lose that, but you still want it to be better. So here are some guiding principles to keep in mind:

- Your goal is a better fit between you and your job. There are a lot of paths you can choose to get to this kind of match, but it is the match that you are after. This goal requires some accommodation from both you and your workplace. After you've implemented a strategy, both you and your job will be a bit different than before.

- The six strategic areas are your guideposts for change. They are the markers for the major sources of burnout, and they frame the strategies for achieving engagement with work. Keep referring back to them as you make progress toward your goal, and use them as a benchmark for your relationship with It.

- Be realistic about the challenges of change and remember the change mantra: "Things will get worse before they get better." There will always be a bumpy road to success, because change involves unfamiliar ways of doing things, which will always disrupt one's life, and of course there are the bugs and glitches that are a normal part of shifting gears. And as we have mentioned throughout this book, there will always be resistance to any kind of change. If you have ever had to remodel your kitchen or fix up another room in your house, then you can fully appreciate how things will be a mess before they are wonderful. So don't be discouraged by the bumps in the road. This is a normal part of the path to change, and you will need to hang in there when the initial going gets tough.

- Keep an eye out for possible ripple effects, which may have an impact on things beyond your original objective. Sometimes these effects prove to have additional benefits. For example, if you start working with people to address issues of disrespect or lack of acknowledgment, you may end up developing a new network of social support and friendship. Sometimes, however, the unintended consequences may be negative. For example, a change in the bookkeeping system, which improves things for the accounting department, may make life more stressful for the salespeople. Try as you might, it is never possible to design the perfect system or to anticipate every single consequence of change—which means that you will always have to be vigilant for the unexpected and prepared to make some adjustments, if necessary.

Telling It Good-bye

If, despite all your best strategic efforts, the relationship between you and It keeps going downhill, then you will have to face a definitive choice: Should I stay, or is it time to move on? You are going to be vulnerable to continuing burnout if the match between you and your job cannot be improved.

Presumably, any mismatch between a person and a job could be resolved, if people and workplaces were infinitely flexible. But that isn't always the case. For example, some organizations are adamant about maintaining central control. They will not permit individual units to set their quarterly profit targets, with the result that setting more reasonable targets cannot be a way of alleviating excessive workload. Another example is a mining company that has firm limits on the amount that it will invest in restoring spoiled landscapes. On the other side of the equation, people have firm limits on the number of hours they are willing to work, or the extent to which they will bend their principles to fit in with their employer's values. When the limits are firm and the mismatch is major, you will need to face the possibility of leaving It for another.

Changing your job is still an occasion for strategic planning. Even though saying, "I quit," and slamming the door may be a great release, it doesn't set up well for finding your next job. A great asset in any job search is already having a job. And there is a lot to be said for taking your time and being picky. The point of leaving this job is to find one that is a better match or at least has the flexibility to become a better match. After all, you probably thought your *current* job was going to work out great when it started!

With the guidance of the six strategies, you now have a better idea of what to seek in a new job. This knowledge is a foundation for carefully examining a new job possibility. It increases the chances that a change will lead to a meaningful improvement.

Let's Do It Again

So onward! You have a plan, you know where you want to go, so stay committed to your goal of improving your relationship with It. As you come to the end of this book, you may think that this is the end of your relationship with us and that you are completely on your own out there. But no! We are ready to stay in touch with you as you proceed on your journey.

- First, this book will continue to be a helpful guide to you in the years to come, as your relationship with It changes and you need to revisit the six strategies for the next phase of your plan. So do keep the book as a constant companion on your bookshelf, so we can reacquaint you with the strategies whenever you need us again.

- Second, after several months, when changes seem to be taking effect, come back to us to check up on your progress. You may have some general sense of how things are going, but testing yourself on the six strategic areas will give you a better picture of whether things are improving. The next section will give you directions on just how to do that.

- Third, we maintain a Web site, CORD.acadiau.ca, where we hope to establish a dialogue with people working through the ideas in this book.

Getting More from Us: CORD.acadiau.ca

Eliminating burnout is a big issue for many people. There are people across the country and around the world with struggles similar to your mismatches at work. There may be a lot to gain from connecting with others, sharing your experiences with the program, and learning about ways in which others have approached these problems.

By visiting this Web site, you can do the following:

- Pose questions.
- Join a discussion group.
- Find up-to-date information on managing burnout.
- Download electronic copies of the forms used in this book.
- Generate a profile comparing your initial profile with your checkup profile.

The site is designed as an ongoing update to the issues in this book. It is a means to build a community of people working to enhance the quality of their work life.

The Web site is maintained by COR&D, the Centre for Organizational Research & Development (COR&D), at Acadia University in Nova Scotia. COR&D is the base for our research and our international work with organizations and individuals. You'll probably be interested in other parts of the Web site, as well as the section supporting this book.

Checking Your Progress

When you are ready to take the My Relationship with Work Test again, you will find a blank new form in the next section of the book, Checking Up. Just like before, answer each question by indicating whether things are just right, or a mismatch, or a major mismatch. The scoring directions will guide you in filling out your new personal profile.

Be sure *not* to look at your old scores first! You do not want to bias your current thinking by bringing back the past. This is not a test with right or wrong answers, but a reflection of how you are feeling about the relationship at this second point in time.

Once you have completed the new profile, then you can compare it with the first profile that you completed several months ago. You should focus on the particular strategy that formed the basis for your action plan. Have your scores on those items moved toward less of a mismatch or even toward being just right? In light of your experience in implementing your action plan, how would you evaluate your current standing in this particular strategic area?

You should also look at the comparison between your current and earlier scores on the other five areas. Sometimes change in one strategic area can have ripple effects in another. For example, an improvement in methods of recognition (reward) may enhance people's willingness to help each other out (community). But it is also the case that other events within your organization will have created some new mismatches, and these may get reflected in your new personal profile. For example, if there have been some unpleasant layoff procedures, as a result of an economic downturn, then you may be experiencing a greater mismatch on fairness and workload.

As we said earlier, a relationship is ongoing and evolving—and it never reaches a steady state of perfect nirvana. That is why it is helpful to check in with the My Relationship with Work Test on a regular basis (like an annual checkup). Some strategic areas will get better—particularly those you have targeted in your action plan—but you should also be prepared for some areas to stay the same or even get worse, depending on the larger social, economic, and political circumstances of the times. The good news is that once again you will be prepared to shift to a new strategy to address your new challenges with It, as a result of taking the test and getting an updated profile.

Conclusion

So banish burnout! And may you and It have a happy and healthy relationship. By building a better relationship with your work, you are demonstrating that a fulfilling work life is possible for you and for others.

Checking Up

It's time to take the My Relationship with Work Test again and see where you stand now that you've implemented the steps in the book.

My Relationship with Work Test

Find out which areas of your work are a match, which areas are a mismatch, and which areas are just right.

- In each of the six areas, how does your current job fit with your preferences, work patterns, and aspirations? If things on a given dimension are just right, put a check in the Just Right column.
- If a certain dimension is incompatible with your preferred way of working, put a check in the Mismatch column.
- If a quality is a major departure from your ideals, put a check in the Major Mismatch column.

Workload

This section is about the work. The items focus on the amount of work, the kind of work, the pace of work, and the demands of work. These items call for a fairly long-term perspective. The issue isn't today's workload but the state of things over the past few months and how you expect things to be in the foreseeable future.

		Just Right	Mismatch	Major Mismatch	Score
	Rating	0	1	2	
W1	The amount of work to complete in a day				
W2	The complexity of my work				
W3	The intensity of demands from customers				
W4	The firmness of deadlines				
W5	The frequency of surprising, unexpected events				
W6	The opportunity to settle into a comfortable groove				
W7	The frequency of interruptions in my workday				
W8	The proportion of my work time spent with customers				
W9	The amount of time I work alone				
W10	The amount of time I work with other employees				
	Workload Total				

Control

This section focuses on the environment for making decisions at work. The items concern the amount of authority you can exercise over your job and over the operation of your work group. For these items, it doesn't matter how you've gained this authority. You may be empowered by company policy or you may have gained influence through your personal networking. The issue is about providing an accurate reading of your capacity to make decisions about your work.

		Just Right	Mismatch	Major Mismatch	Score
	Rating	0	1	2	
C1	The amount of group decision making in my work setting				
C2	The extent to which I share authority with coworkers				
C3	The amount of information my supervisor provides on major developments in the organization				
C4	My participation in decisions that affect my work				
C5	The quality of leadership from upper management				
C6	The quality of leadership shown by my immediate supervisor				
C7	The authority I am assigned in my area of responsibility				
C8	Opportunities to exercise my professional judgment				
C9	My capacity to influence decisions that affect my work				
C10	My freedom to follow my professional judgment				
	Control Total				

Reward

This section is about rewards. There are many ways a job can be rewarding and just as many ways that it can miss the boat. For this section, give some thought to the sorts of things that keep you going.

		Just Right	Mismatch	Major Mismatch	Score
	Rating	0	1	2	
R1	My salary and benefits relative to what I require				
R2	My salary and benefits relative to what I could get elsewhere				
R3	Recognition for achievements from my supervisor				
R4	Recognition for achievements from management other than my supervisor				
R5	The rigorousness of regular performance evaluations				
R6	My access to perks at work—travel, office furniture, conference support, and so forth				
R7	Opportunities for promotion				
R8	Opportunities for bonuses or raises				
R9	The amount of time I do work I truly enjoy				
R10	The amount of time I work with people I truly enjoy				
	Reward Total				

Community

The focus in this section is the people who make up your *social work environment* (hence the designation S on the test, which distinguishes it from the C used in the control section). Think of the people you encounter on the job: clients, coworkers, bosses, subordinates, and others.

		Just Right	Mismatch	Major Mismatch	Score
	Rating	0	1	2	
S1	The ease of discovering what is happening across the organization				
S2	Open, honest communication across the organization				
S3	The freedom to express differences of opinion				
S4	The extent people must rely on others at work				
S5	The frequency of supportive interactions at work				
S6	The closeness of personal friendships at work				
S7	The amount people interact informally at work				
S8	A shared sense of purpose across the organization				
S9	My sense of community with the entire organization				
S10	The extent of openness to people from units other than one's own				
	Community Total				

Fairness

This section focuses on respect and fairness. Think of the important decisions that affect the quality of your work life. How are people around you treated, and how do you treat others? To what extent are fairness and respect evident in the life of your company?

	Just Right	Mismatch	Major Mismatch	Score
Rating	0	1	2	
F1 My supervisor's attention to treating employees fairly				
F2 Upper management's attention to treating employees fairly				
F3 Management's dedication to giving everyone equal consideration				
F4 Clear and open procedures for allocating rewards and promotions				
F5 Procedures for discipline that are specified in detail				
F6 The objectivity of decisions on pay raises or bonuses				
F7 The objectivity of decisions on work schedules and assignments				
F8 The extent to which individuals interact politely and respectfully				
F9 The level of cultural sensitivity across the organization				
F10 The organization's accommodation of diverse backgrounds and abilities				
Fairness Total				

Values

Do you believe in what you're doing? This section is about the way your values and those of your company fit together. Or don't. Think of the crunch issues that pit one set of values against another. Does the company come through for you? Does the company come through for its own corporate values?

		Just Right	Mismatch	Major Mismatch	Score
	Rating	0	1	2	
V1	The depth of management's commitment to its mission				
V2	The influence of organizational values on my work				
V3	The influence of the organization's values in everything it does				
V4	The level of honesty across the organization				
V5	Management's diligence in maintaining honesty and integrity				
V6	My willingness to make personal sacrifices in order to further my organization's mission				
V7	The potential of my work to contribute to the larger community				
V8	My confidence that the organization's mission is meaningful				
V9	The constructive impact of the organization's mission and activities				
V10	The organization's contribution to improving the general quality of life				
	Values Total				
	Grand Total				

Scoring

Scoring the test gives you a Total for each of the six strategic areas. Here's what you do:

- For each of the six sections, put a check in the cell under either Just Right, Mismatch, or Major Mismatch for each item. Then enter the Rating number (0, 1, or 2) into the right-hand Score column for each item.

- Add up the scores within each strategic area and put the total score in the Total cell. This will give you six Total scores, one for each strategic area.

- In the Grand Total row at the bottom of the test, enter the sum of the six Total scores and then divide by six.

Profile

Now you have the information to plot your personal profile, which will provide the strategic direction for your action plan.

For each of the six Total Scores, find the corresponding number on the scale along the left side of the graph (see figure that follows). Fill in the rectangle for each strategic area to the height corresponding to the score. The score can range from a low of 0 (indicating everything is just right) to a high of 20, indicating a major mismatch on every item for that particular strategic area. See the following graph.

Checking Your Progress

Compare this new profile with the profile you completed at the beginning of the process. Improvements are shown by the lines going lower, because the length of the line represents the seriousness of your mismatch.

- Is the decrease in the area of work life on which you've been focusing your strategy? If so, keep it up. It's working!

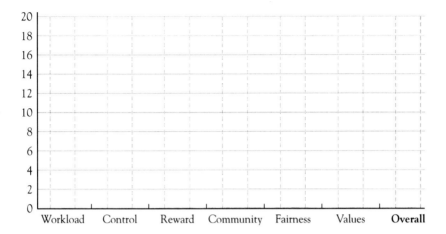

- Is the decrease in other areas of work life? If so, then your strategies are having a broader-than-expected effect.

  Increased levels on the lines indicate that you're losing ground.

- Is the increase in the area of work life on which you've been focusing your strategy? If so, your strategy needs fine-tuning or even a major overhaul.
- Is the increase in other areas of work life? If so, your strategies may be creating unintended problems in other aspects of your work life. It is time to consider your situation and your strategy in a broader context.

Web Site Information

We invite you to visit the Web site supporting this book at CORD.acadiau.ca.

By visiting this Web site, you can do the following:

- Pose questions.
- Join a discussion group.
- Find up-to-date information on managing burnout.
- Download electronic copies of the forms used in this book.
- Generate a profile comparing your initial profile with your checkup profile.

The site is designed as an ongoing update to the issues in this book. It is a means to build a community of people working to enhance the quality of their work life.

The Web site is maintained by the Centre for Organizational Research & Development (COR&D) at Acadia University in Nova Scotia. COR&D is the base for our research and our international work with organizations and individuals. You'll probably be interested in other parts of the Web site, as well as the section supporting this book.

About the Authors

Michael P. Leiter is professor of psychology at Acadia University in Canada and director of the Center for Organizational Research & Development, which applies high-quality research methods to human resource issues that confront organizations. He holds the Canada Research Chair in Occupational Health and Wellness at Acadia University.

He received degrees in psychology from Duke University (bachelor's), Vanderbilt University (master's), and the University of Oregon (doctorate). He teaches courses on organizational psychology and on stress at Acadia University. The research center provides a lively bridge between university studies and organizational consultation for Leiter and his students.

Leiter has received ongoing research funding for twenty years from the Social Sciences and Humanities Research Council of Canada as well as from international foundations. He is actively involved as a consultant on occupational issues in Canada, the United States, and Europe. Through the Centre for Organizational Research & Development, he has fine-tuned a capacity for survey research, which has resulted in major research projects, new approaches to data analysis, and the publication of new survey measures. This approach to organizational life arose from his extensive work with organizations that were undergoing major organizational change in North America and in Europe.

Christina Maslach is professor of psychology and the vice provost for undergraduate education at the University of California, Berkeley.

She has conducted research in social and health psychology and is best known as a pioneering researcher on job burnout and as the author of the widely used Maslach Burnout Inventory (MBI). She has written numerous articles and books, including *Burnout: The Cost of Caring;* the coedited volume *Professional Burnout: Recent Developments in Theory and Research;* and two prior books with Michael Leiter, *The Truth About Burnout* and *Preventing Burnout and Building Engagement.*

Maslach's research accomplishments led the American Association for the Advancement of Science to honor her "for groundbreaking work on the applications of social psychology to contemporary problems." She is also a renowned teacher who received national recognition and was named Carnegie Foundation Professor of the Year in 1997. She received her bachelor of arts degree, magna cum laude, in social relations from Harvard-Radcliffe College, and her doctorate in psychology from Stanford University.

Maslach's academic career was actually her second choice; she originally intended to become a professional ballet dancer. She maintains her passion for the performing and fine arts and tries to keep her life filled with as much of them as possible.

Index

CPSIA information can be obtained at www.ICGtesting.com
Printed in the USA
LVOW11s2139190214

374456LV00002B/132/P